Oliver Tambo

JACANA POCKET SERIES

The new series of Jacana pocket guides is meant for those who are looking for a brief but lively introduction to a wide range of topics of African history, politics and biography, written by some of the leading experts in their fields.

Govan Mbeki, Colin Bundy

Nelson Mandela, Colin Bundy

Short-changed: SA since Apartheid, Colin Bundy

The Idea of the ANC, Anthony Butler

Umkhonto weSizwe, Janet Cherry

South Africa's Struggle for Human Rights, Saul Dubow

The ANC Youth League, Clive Glaser

Thomas Sankara, Ernest Harsch

The ANC Women's League, Shireen Hassim

Frantz Fanon, Christopher J. Lee

San Rock Art, J.D. Lewis-Williams

Chris Hani, Hugh Macmillan

Jack Simons, Hugh Macmillan

Oliver Tambo, Hugh Macmillan

South Africa at War, 1939–45, Bill Nasson

The Soweto Uprising, Noor Nieftagodien

Patrice Lumumba, Georges Nzongola-Ntalaja

Plague, Pox and Pandemics, Howard Phillips

Haile Selassie, Bereket Habte Selassie

Ingrid Jonker, Louise Viljoen

Steve Biko, Lindy Wilson

Shaka, Dan Wylie

Oliver Tambo

A Jacana
pocket biography

Hugh Macmillan

First published by Jacana Media (Pty) Ltd in 2017

10 Orange Street
Sunnyside
Auckland Park 2092
South Africa
+2711 628 3200
www.jacana.co.za

ISBN 978-1-4314-2563-1

Cover design by publicide
Set in Minion 10/14.5pt
Printed and bound by Bidvest Data
Job no. 003058

See a complete list of Jacana titles at www.jacana.co.za

Contents

1

The early years, 1917–41

Oliver Reginald Kaisana Tambo, who came to be known as 'OR', but was also known to some as 'Bones', from the English translation of his isiXhosa surname, was born at Kantolo (now Nkantolo) near Bizana (now Mbizana) in Eastern Pondoland, then part of the Transkeian Territories, now part of the Eastern Cape, on 27 October 1917 – his birth coincided almost exactly with Russia's October Revolution. He was born during the fourth year of the First World War, and his father, Mzimeni, also known by his clan name as 'Manchi', in what may have been a mildly rebellious gesture, named him after the German Kaiser, who was Great Britain's and the Union of South Africa's opponent in the war. Tambo's near contemporary, Kaiser Matanzima, who became the Transkei Bantustan leader, had been similarly named in the previous year.

Kaisana acquired his English names, Oliver Reginald, and his surname, which was derived from 'Thambo', his grandfather's first name, when he started school at the age of five or six. Unlike Matanzima's father or Nelson Mandela's, Mzimeni had no place in the 'traditional' hierarchy, nor was he formally educated. He had arrived in the neighbourhood of Kantolo with his parents and several siblings in the mid-1890s, crossing the Engeli Mountains from the Harding district of Natal at about the same time that Eastern and Western Pondoland were formally annexed to the Cape Colony by Prime Minister Cecil John Rhodes in 1894.

Pondoland was one of the last parts of South Africa to lose its independence and had been under colonial rule for little more than twenty years when Oliver Tambo was born. The Transkeian Territories formed the largest block of land in African ownership in South Africa – significantly larger and more populous than either Basutoland (Lesotho) or Swaziland. The settlement at Kantolo is close to a tributary of the Umtamvuna River, which reaches the Indian Ocean on the Wild Coast, and is about sixteen kilometres north-west of Bizana. It took its name from the post office (*poskantoor* in Afrikaans) that was attached to the local Ntlazukazi Trading Store, which was run for many years by the Mountjoy family.

The family's homestead was a large one, which Mzimeni shared with his parents while they lived, and later with his three brothers and their families. Following the trader's example, he had an enclosed garden with fruit trees where he grew vegetables. He cultivated maize or millet with the help of his wives – one of them died young and there were never more than three at one time – and his nine children. At the height of his prosperity in the mid-1920s, he had about fifty cattle and some horses, which grazed on the surrounding common land, and an ox-wagon, with which he carried on a transport business.

Mzimeni may not have been formally educated, but he was an entrepreneur. He had worked for a while as an assistant at the local store and admired the wealth and status that the local trader achieved. He attributed these qualities to literacy and numeracy, skills that he was determined that his children should acquire. His third wife, Julia, who was Oliver's mother, appears to have been born to a Christian family and was literate. The whole family was in 1930 influenced by an evangelical and Pentecostal campaign by what became known as the Full Gospel Church – it was then that Mzimeni himself became a Christian.

By the late 1920s or early 1930s the family, which had been relatively prosperous, was impoverished, probably as a result of two consecutive drought years in 1926 and 1927, which affected crops, livestock and the transport business, and then by the onset in 1929 of the Great Depression, which overshadowed Oliver Tambo's secondary school years. The income of the homestead as a whole had been supplemented by the involvement of some of its members, including Mzimeni's brothers and his elder sons, in labour migration to the coal mines and plantations of Natal.

In October 1926, shortly before Oliver's ninth birthday, the family received the news of the deaths in a mining disaster of Mzimeni's brother Mbizweni (Oliver's uncle) and his son James (Zakhele), one of Oliver's elder brothers. They were among the 124 victims of a methane gas explosion and fire at the Durban Navigation No. 2 Colliery at Dannhauser in northern Natal. This tragedy, which still ranks today as one of the worst disasters in the history of coal mining in South Africa, demonstrated the evils of the migrant labour system and had a lifelong impact on Tambo. Sixty years later, he could not hear the news of a mining accident without being reminded of the loss that his family had then suffered. The compensation payable for the loss of a black life was, he recalled, only £30. His uncle had just married and left a widow and a small child.

Oliver Tambo was most unusual among black South Africans who went on to higher education in the 1930s in that he came from not only a rural but what might be described as a 'peasant' background. In her biography of Professor Z.K. Matthews, Monica Wilson identified him as one of only four such students to reach Fort Hare University College in that decade. The great majority of the black students who reached university then came, like Nelson Mandela and the Matanzima brothers, from royal or chiefly families, or from middle-class families that had several generations of Christianity and literacy behind them.

Oliver began his education at the local primary school, which was run by the Methodist Church, and then moved to one at Emobheni, about fifteen kilometres away from home, to which he sometimes travelled daily on foot or on horseback, and where he was, for a while, a weekly boarder. It was at that school that he was introduced to tonic sol-fa and began to develop his lifelong interest in music. As a small child he owned neither shoes nor trousers, and wore a wrap-around cloth and a blanket. He bore scarifications on his cheeks, which identified him as Pondo, did his share of cattle herding, and was an adept at stick fighting. But he became one of a long line of devoutly religious leaders of the African National Congress (ANC), which began with Dr John Dube and included Tambo's immediate predecessor as president, Chief Albert Luthuli.

In his earliest memoir, which was recorded by his friend and mentor, Father (later Archbishop) Trevor Huddleston, in 1954, he gave this account of an early crisis in his educational history: 'I went to a mission primary school, but when I got to Standard Four I began to play truant. School was boring to me and I just stopped going. By that time my father was old and had lost all his wealth; he was a farmer and he was just unfortunate. We were terribly poor. I thought of going out to work. It was

11

at that moment in my life that the first great change and chance occurred.'

By Huddleston's account a priest, or by Tambo's later account a family friend, visited his father from the Anglican Holy Cross Mission and suggested that Oliver and a brother should return with him to board at the mission school. Tambo gave Huddleston his own account of what was clearly a decisive moment in his life: 'I arrived there on Easter Day, with one of my stepbrothers, and I shall never forget that moment. We entered the great church while the Mass of Easter was being sung. I can still see the red cassocks of the servers, the grey smoke of the incense, the vestments of the priests at the altar … it was a new world.'

The five years that Oliver spent at Holy Cross Mission would not have been possible without a donation of £6 a year, several hundred pounds a year in today's money, from two sisters in England, the Misses Joyce and Ruth Goddard, and a similar contribution from his elder brother Willy, who worked as a labour migrant. Huddleston later made contact with the Goddard sisters, who had kept an archive of all Tambo's thank-you letters and other letters from the school relating to his progress. Among them is the first of his letters, which was written on 27 October 1928, his eleventh birthday. In this remarkable letter, he thanked the sisters for their support, and told them that he had recently been baptised by the visiting bishop, and that he was about to do his Standard Four exams. He wondered whether the inspector would be very strict and asked for their prayers.

He seems to have had to repeat the year as he did not proceed to Standard Five until 1930. He completed Standard Six and primary school in 1931, but was then compelled to repeat the year twice, though with some more advanced work, while waiting for a place at secondary school. He was unable to secure sufficient funding for a place at St John's College in Umtata or at Mariannhill, a Catholic school in Natal. It was only at the end of 1933 that he was saved by the intervention of Archdeacon Leary, a priest at Holy Cross, who helped him to get a place at the Anglican Community of the Resurrection's St Peter's School in Rosettenville, Johannesburg. The Goddard sisters continued to support him throughout his school career, but they could not provide for all his needs, nor could his brother Willy.

In January 1934 he set off with his friend Robert Sonqishe on the long journey by bus from Bizana to Kokstad, and by train from there to the Witwatersrand. It is not difficult to imagine the impact of their first sight of this massive mining industrial complex on fifteen-year-old boys from deeply rural Pondoland. He later recalled their unfamiliarity with the notion of a horse-drawn cab plying for hire. Their school contemporaries recalled that they arrived at school, country-style, with their shoes tied around their necks. But it was also the first time that, coming from the Transkei, they were exposed to racial segregation, as at Johannesburg's Park Station, and overt racism.

Although he was used to the ethos of Anglicanism, St Peter's was also different. It was run by monks of the Community of the Resurrection – an order that had been founded by Bishop Charles Gore, who was also the founder of the Christian Social Union. The Community was not only High Church – that is to say Anglo-Catholic – but also strongly influenced by the ideals of Christian socialism as initially promoted by F.D. Maurice and, later on, by Bishop Gore himself. Above all, St Peter's was urban and cosmopolitan, drawing pupils from all over the country. By contrast with Holy Cross where isiXhosa was the common language of the pupils, the lingua franca at St Peter's was English. Tambo later realised that the two frustrating years, during which he had to repeat Standard Six, had been useful, as he had then done some secondary school work and this gave him a slight advantage over his contemporaries.

In his first two years at St Peter's, he received the news of the deaths of both his parents. His mother died in September 1934 – he did not receive the news until November – and his father died in September of the following year. Oliver had been able to return home in June 1934 and had then seen his mother for the last time. It was on that visit that he demonstrated his leadership potential, becoming one of the founders of a short-lived Bizana Students Association. He later recalled that the death of his parents had deprived him for a while of motivation. He had always hoped that he would be able to do something to improve his parents' standard of living, but regretted that he had only ever been able to contribute ten shillings, which he had earned from a holiday job at Holy Cross six years previously, to the household income. He recalled that his younger mother, Lena, took over responsibility for the family, and that she was an 'absolutely wonderful' woman.

Oliver soon demonstrated that he was not just a bright student, but one of the cleverest pupils in the country. When his class wrote the Junior Certificate exams at the end of 1938 – at a time when black and white pupils wrote the same exams – he and his companion Joe Mokoena were the first two black pupils in the Transvaal to be placed in the first class, first division, indicating average marks in all subjects of over 80 per cent. They had achieved distinctions in maths, science, Latin and history.

As a result of his success in these exams, Tambo was awarded a scholarship worth £30 a year for five years by the Bhunga – the Transkei General Council – and a further £20 a year by the University of South Africa. These scholarships helped to see him through his later years at school and university. It was also at St Peter's that Tambo began to impress his peers as a debater and his teachers as a potential leader. But he also displayed a degree of reticence that was to remain one of his notable characteristics. When he was asked to be head prefect in his final year, he declined the invitation and suggested that he should be deputy head – in much the same way that he seems later to have preferred the posts of deputy or acting president of the ANC to the substantive post. In the matriculation exams at the end of 1938, he was again placed in the first class with a distinction in maths. His friend Joe Mokoena managed three distinctions.

He would have liked to study medicine at university, as he had a special interest in investigating the healing properties of African herbs. But it was not then possible for black students to study medicine in South Africa and there was no possibility of his finding the funds to study abroad. He showed a measure of academic self-confidence in choosing to do the BSc degree in what were regarded as the most difficult subjects – maths and physics – while most BSc students, of whom there were very few, chose what were thought to be the easier options of chemistry and zoology. He always regretted, however, that he had been unable to study subjects such as philosophy, sociology and law at university. He was, of course, to go on later to train as a lawyer.

Entry to Fort Hare University College took Tambo back to the Eastern Cape. He became a member of Beda Hall, a newly built Anglican hall of residence, which had a distinctly ecumenical flavour. Its founding warden, Bishop Smyth, welcomed Catholic as well as Hindu and Muslim students. Tambo later commented on his religious life at this time: 'After my encounter with evangelists of …

the Full Gospel Church at my home in or around 1930, my religious life took on a new and more personalised character. I developed a liking for the early morning Holy Communion service that would normally be held in a chapel, which, because it was early, attracted few people. Often I was the only one attending. But if there was no service, I went to the chapel anyway for prayers, if not in the morning, then at any time of the day … Being at Beda Hall provided me personally with the facility that I had enjoyed both at Holy Cross Mission and at St Peter's Secondary School – that was the Chapel.'

Tambo had begun to develop at school and university a deep 'hinterland' in the related spheres of religion and music, which was to be a source of great strength to him in his later political and exile life. At Fort Hare he led the Beda Hall Double Quartet, which sang 'Negro spirituals and Bantu songs'. During one vacation he organised a prize-winning choir on a return visit to Holy Cross and composed three songs for a concert in honour of Archdeacon Leary's retirement. In ensuing decades and in exile, he never missed an opportunity to take charge of a choir and was, as will be shown later, supportive of the ANC's cultural activities, including the Amandla Cultural Ensemble.

Tambo was clearly an industrious student who got a good BSc degree with a distinction in maths in 1941. He had become a total, and lifelong, abstainer from alcohol at the age of sixteen and was, apparently, a celibate student. His closest friends included Congress Mbatha, later an academic in the United States and a leader of the ANC; Lancelot Gama, who became a medical doctor; and Joe Mokoena, his contemporary from St Peter's, who went on to do postgraduate work at the University of the Witwatersrand and in the United States. Mokoena taught mathematics at Fort Hare and at universities in Ghana and Nigeria, but died as a result of a car accident in Lusaka while teaching at the University of Zambia in 1969.

Although Tambo usually appeared to be modest and at times reticent, Joe Matthews, the young son of Professor Z.K. Matthews, a prominent black member of the academic staff and later acting principal, recalled him from Fort Hare as argumentative and loquacious. He was a competent sportsman, playing football and cricket for his hall. Nelson Mandela, an outstanding sportsman, recalled first meeting him on the football field, and thought of him as unusually political for a science student. His sporting career may have been terminated by his first attack of asthma in 1940. He had previously been thought on two occasions to have tuberculosis, but this seems not to have been confirmed.

He was always a first-class debater and emerged as a student leader, serving on the Students Representative Council (SRC) in 1941 as the representative of his hall. He played a prominent part in negotiations around a student strike in that year, which was ended as a result of the intervention of Z.K. Matthews. In his postgraduate year, while doing the diploma in education in 1942, Tambo was not only the head student at Beda Hall, but was also unanimously elected, on the basis of his performance in the previous year, as secretary of the SRC. These two positions led him into a decisive conflict with the authorities within two months of his final exams.

There was a dispute about whether a tennis court at Beda Hall, which had been refurbished by student labour through Tambo's own initiative, could be used on a Sunday. This resulted in a student strike during which Tambo was the lead negotiator. Professor Matthews saw this as a struggle for control between the students and the warden, and proposed mediation by the Archbishop of Cape Town. The warden rejected mediation, which Tambo had accepted on behalf of the students, and demanded an immediate end to the strike and a solemn pledge of future good behaviour. Tambo was, typically, both resolute and flexible. He encouraged students who were about to write the final exams for their first degrees to return to classes, but he decided that he could not make the pledge. As he told Father Huddleston: 'I asked the warden for time to pray about this, and I went to the chapel for half an hour. I knew I could not sign that pledge. It would have killed my religion stone dead – an agreement with God, written and sealed. I could not do it.'

As a result of this determination he was expelled and had to leave Fort Hare without a teaching diploma. As he recalled: 'I wandered into Alice and stayed there till nightfall. I just did not see what I could do. I decided, anyhow, to go back to the chapel and pray. So at eleven o' clock that night I opened the door. It was completely dark, absolutely silent. But at the far end, near the Blessed Sacrament, there was a glow of light from the lamp that always burned there. I took that as a sign. That somewhere, however dark, there is a light …'

In a despairing mood, he returned home and contemplated going to Durban to look for a menial job. At the last minute he received an offer from his old school, St Peter's, which found, unexpectedly, that it had the funds for an additional teacher of science and higher mathematics. So he returned from the Eastern Cape to Johannesburg, and a new chapter in his life opened.

2

Johannesburg and the ANC Youth League, 1943–50

Although he was active in student politics, there is no evidence that Oliver Tambo had any involvement in national politics while he was at Fort Hare. The ANC, which had been at a low ebb for most of the 1930s, had no presence on the campus. It was only following the election of Dr A.B. Xuma as president of the ANC in 1940 that the organisation began to revive. This revival coincided with the outbreak of the Second World War, which occurred during Tambo's first year at Fort Hare. The ANC under Xuma supported South Africa's participation in the war. In the memoir that he dictated in 1987–8, Tambo indicated that he and his fellow students took a keen interest in the war. He also indicated, however, a measure of ambivalence about a war in which his own brother Alan took part from 1939 to 1945. In his later memoirs, he recalled the experience of black soldiers during the First World War: 'During that war, hundreds of Africans danced their way to death on the decks of their ship known as the Mendi ... They died most gallantly. That drama became a household story among the Africans, kept alive by the reality that although the war was won, far from improving, our conditions worsened. The persistent question, "What did the Mendi heroes die for?" had not been answered as General Smuts's men went around recruiting for the Second World War.'

He also recalled his attendance at a recruitment meeting at Qumbu in the Transkei, probably in 1940, and the scepticism of the audience about a government which, having disarmed the African population and taken its land, was now calling upon the same people to help defend the country against Hitler, while refusing to allow them to carry guns.

As the country's only black university college, Fort Hare was a national institution and Tambo's reputation as a student leader preceded him to Johannesburg. On a visit to the city during the long vacation, early in 1942, he had, with his friends Congress Mbatha and Lancelot Gama, been introduced to Walter Sisulu, another Transkeian, who had, most unusually, set himself up as an estate agent with an office in the centre of the town. Although he lacked much formal education, Sisulu was a person of great intelligence and drive who would eventually emerge, with Tambo and Mandela, as one of a triumvirate of key leaders of both the ANC Youth League and the ANC itself.

On Tambo's return to Johannesburg to start work in 1943, he found that his reputation had been enhanced as a result of the part that he played in the Beda Hall strike. This had attracted a great deal of publicity nationally and had prompted sympathetic interventions by the 'non-European' trade unions and by the liberal Institute of Race Relations. It had also been discussed at the ANC conference in Bloemfontein in December 1942. The issue was raised by Tambo's close friend Lancelot Gama, who suggested the formation of a youth league within the ANC. This proposal was approved by the conference in principle. Gama would not have made the suggestion without consulting Tambo, and so it is reasonable to say that they jointly sowed the seed from which the ANC Youth League emerged over the next eighteen months.

The year 1943 was important for Tambo for at least three reasons. It marked the beginning of his five-year career as a teacher at St Peter's; it was the year in which he met Father Trevor Huddleston, who had just arrived to join the Community of the Resurrection in Johannesburg; and it was the year in which he had his first real contact with the ANC, which was to dominate his life for the next fifty years.

Tambo was remembered by his former students as an effective teacher of maths and physics. Joe Matthews, who became his pupil, thought that he adopted the teaching methods of one of the more challenging of his Fort Hare lecturers. Another pupil recalled his insistence on the need for logical thinking – a quality that shines through Tambo's own letters and memoranda. His pupils also remembered him as a strict disciplinarian who was not opposed to corporal punishment and was an effective wielder of the cane – something that was very much part of the British and colonial education system at that time. He became an active member of the Transvaal African Teachers Association and participated in their march through Johannesburg in 1944. Known to both his pupils and fellow staff as 'Brother T' or 'Bra T', he was a highly respected teacher and the successful organiser of the school choir.

Father Trevor Huddleston

The friendship between Tambo and Huddleston was hugely important to both men. In a letter that he wrote to Huddleston many years later, he recalled the impact of the latter's arrival in 'racist South Africa, my motherland'. One of his colleagues had said: 'this new priest that has arrived at St Cyprian's should prove to be just what our people need – a man who is prepared to work with the people – this might prove to be a worthy find.' As he recalled: 'You arrived armed with truth as your sword and integrity as your breastplate and ready to follow the Master to the cross if necessary.' Tambo's future wife, Adelaide, who also met Huddleston at this time, remembered that he became 'a religious model to Oliver. He conducted himself as a priest in a manner that Oliver would have liked to emulate, working among the people.' There can be little doubt that it was Tambo, more than any other individual, who inspired Huddleston to take a political stand against apartheid, and it was Huddleston, more than any other individual, who inspired Tambo to seek ordination in the mid-1950s in the Church of the Province of South Africa – the Anglican Church. In a letter that he wrote a few months before his death, Tambo said that he wished: 'to stress that nothing is more precious to me than our unbroken friendship over fifty years … I cannot say how much we value your consistent support and clarity of mind about our political situation. It will remain a shining force of example long after we have gone. The immortality of it all will be emblazoned on the grave of apartheid …'

Huddleston recalled in his address at the requiem mass for Tambo in Johannesburg in April 1993 that Tambo had not only given him the gift of friendship, but had enabled him to recognise 'the fundamental truth about the consequences – political, economic, social, cultural and theological – of South Africa's ideological philosophy. Apartheid.' He had not learnt the meaning of apartheid by academic study. 'I learnt it in the streets and homes and schools of Sophiatown and Orlando. I learnt it from the people whose parish priest I was and for whom, under God, I had pastoral responsibility.'

The ANC and the Youth League

Through his friendship with Walter Sisulu, Tambo became a frequent visitor to the home of the ANC's president, Dr Xuma, who gathered a group of young graduates – he later called them his 'kindergarten' – around him. As well as Tambo and the non-graduate Sisulu, they included Joe Mokoena, Tambo's friend from St Peter's and Fort Hare; Congress Mbatha, another friend from both those institutions and a fellow teacher at St Peter's; Anton Lembede, A.P. Mda and Nelson Mandela, all law students and articled clerks; Jordan Ngubane, a journalist; and Willie Nkomo, a medical student at the University of the Witwatersrand. Tambo later recalled with approval the way in which Xuma delegated work and involved these young intellectuals, including himself, in drafting letters and memoranda – something that influenced his own way of working as president of the ANC in exile.

Tambo was not a member of the drafting committee, but he may, with some of the other young people around Xuma, have had some input into the production of the two documents, an essay on the Atlantic Charter, which had been signed by F.D. Roosevelt and Winston Churchill in 1941, and a 'Bill of Rights', that came to be known collectively as *Africans' Claims*. They were adopted by the ANC conference at Bloemfontein in December 1943. The statement on the Atlantic Charter restated the right of self-determination, which had been among President Woodrow Wilson's Fourteen Points; demanded the restoration of independence to Abyssinia (Ethiopia); and rejected the prevailing notion of 'trusteeship' by colonial powers.

The Bill of Rights was the most radical document that the ANC had ever produced. It made an explicit demand on behalf of the Africans of South Africa for 'full citizenship rights and direct participation in all the councils of the state'. It also demanded the repeal of all racially discriminatory legislation, including the two Land Acts, the pass laws, the 'Colour Bar' Act, the Masters and Servants Act, and the Natives Labour Regulation Act. It concluded: 'In short, we demand the repeal of any and all laws as well as the abandonment of any policy and all practices that discriminate against the African in any way whatsoever on the basis of race, creed or colour in the Union of South Africa.'

This conference also adopted a new constitution for the ANC, which abolished the House of Chiefs and established the branch as the basic unit of organisation. It also provided for the establishment of a National Working Committee (NWC), composed of five members of the National Executive Committee (NEC) living within eighty kilometres of Johannesburg. Although no effort was made to recruit non-Africans, it did not restrict membership to Africans and it allowed women full membership, not just associate membership, for the first time. It provided for the establishment of a Women's League and it confirmed the previous year's resolution on the formation of a Youth League.

Dr Xuma thought that the NEC should take the initiative about this, and was taken aback when a deputation including Tambo, Sisulu, Ngubane, Mda and Nkomo visited him at his house in Sophiatown in February 1944 and presented him with a draft manifesto and constitution for the Youth League. He did not approve of the 'Africanism' of the manifesto, which appears to have been drafted by Lembede, Ngubane and Mda, and he was afraid that the Youth League was setting itself up in competition with the ANC, but, somewhat reluctantly, he gave the go-ahead for its establishment. Tambo did not attend the inaugural meeting on Easter Day, 9 April 1944, at which he was elected to the provisional committee, but he did participate in the inaugural conference in September 1944. Following Dr Xuma and R.V. Selope Thema, an ANC founder and a distinguished journalist, among others, Tambo gave the last of eight keynote speeches on 'Our Congress Youth League'. He was elected as secretary, while Anton Lembede was elected president, replacing Willie Nkomo, who had acted provisionally in that capacity, and A.P. Mda became vice-president. After Lembede's sudden death in July 1947, Mda succeeded him as president.

Oliver Tambo was not a primary author of the Youth

League's manifesto, but he clearly subscribed to its underlying philosophy, which was one of 'Africanism': that '[the African] NOW ELECTS TO DETERMINE HIS FUTURE BY HIS OWN EFFORTS' and that 'self-determination is the philosophy of life which will save [the African] from the disasters to which Discrimination, Segregation, Pass Laws and Trusteeship are inevitably driving him'. In what must have been the first reference in an ANC document to the 'national liberation movement', the manifesto stated that African Youth was 'LAYING ITS SERVICES AT THE DISPOSAL OF THE NATIONAL LIBERATION MOVEMENT, THE AFRICAN NATIONAL CONGRESS, IN THE FIRM BELIEF, KNOWLEDGE AND CONVICTION THAT THE CAUSE OF AFRICA MUST AND WILL TRIUMPH'. While acknowledging that it might be useful to borrow from 'foreign ideologies', the manifesto stated that 'we reject the wholesale importation of foreign ideologies into Africa'.

The constitution of the Youth League differed from the newly adopted constitution of the ANC itself, which was not specific about race, in stating that membership was open only to 'African men and women' between the ages of twelve and forty. In what may have been a concession to people of mixed race, including Walter Sisulu, it opened the door to members of other sections of the community 'who live like and with Africans and whose general outlook on life is similar to that of Africans'.

Nationalism and exclusivism

Oliver Tambo came to be closely associated in exile with the notion of the ANC as a 'broad church', with room for people of all racial, ethnic and political groupings, but this was a position that he reached gradually after a period of what Sisulu described as 'sharp' nationalism, during which he rejected cooperation with other racial groups, including Indians, and other political groups, including communists. For people who recall Tambo as the mild-mannered and studious leader of the ANC in exile, it is surprising to find that as a young man he had been ready to join Nelson Mandela and others in heckling and breaking up meetings.

He was always, however, flexible and pragmatic. In September 1944, the month of the inaugural conference of the Youth League, he joined the Johannesburg Joint Council of Natives and Europeans, an essentially liberal and non-racial, or multiracial, organisation, of which Dr Xuma had been a member since his return to South Africa in 1930.

In 1945 Lembede, Mandela, Sisulu and Tambo proposed at a conference of the Transvaal ANC that members who were also members of other political parties should resign from them or forfeit their membership of the ANC. They were unable, however, to get this motion, which was clearly aimed at the Communist Party of South Africa (CPSA),and the more or less Trotskyite All African

Convention (AAC) but was opposed by Xuma and other senior members, passed at the ANC's annual conference.

The Youth League was, in 1946, supportive of the African Mine Workers Union, in which black communists, such as J.B. Marks, played a leading role, and of its strike action. After the Smuts government's brutal suppression of the strike, it campaigned for a boycott of the Natives Representative Council – the so-called toy telephone – on which some senior ANC members sat. But in the following year it introduced a motion in the Transvaal ANC to exclude members of other parties from holding office in the ANC – this was narrowly defeated.

It may be that the strong line that Mandela and Tambo and, to a lesser extent, Sisulu took on this issue was driven not so much by ideological or racial exclusivism as by organisational competitiveness. They were determined to build the ANC as 'the national liberation movement'. They did not want to be forced to compete with other organisations for African support. In an interview with Brian Bunting, biographer of Moses Kotane, in the 1970s, Tambo explained his opposition to dual membership of the ANC and the CPSA in these terms: 'At that time I was opposed to some of the positions taken by the Party, and I had the utmost fear of a kind of Party–non-Party situation developing among the membership.' His fear that joint membership could be divisive was tempered by his observation of the behaviour of Moses Kotane at the ANC conferences in 1945 and 1946. 'To my surprise I noticed that Moses did not argue as a Party person at all, but simply went for the facts. I felt that the attitudes some of us had developed about the Party were completely unjustifiable. If it was possible for a leading member of the Party like Moses to speak as he did … I failed to see any difference, and forever afterwards I felt and I said that, if Moses represents the Party, I don't think I will quarrel with it.' He was then able to cooperate with individual communists, but his and Mandela's opposition to the Party as an organisation continued until it was banned in June 1950.

There was also some movement on the part of the leaders of the Youth League, and on Tambo's part, in their approach to cooperation with individual leaders of other racial groups. After Lembede's death, the Youth League, under the leadership of A.P. Mda, shifted its position from 'Africanism' towards African nationalism and, in a revised version of its manifesto, rejected any notion of 'Africa for the Africans'. Lembede himself seems to have moderated his position shortly before his death and was supportive of the 'Xuma-Dadoo-Naicker Pact', which was concluded in March 1947, between the leaders of the ANC and the Transvaal and Natal Indian Congresses.

In the following year, however, the Transvaal ANC was split over the issue of whether to participate in, or to disrupt, the 'Votes for all' campaign, which was led by Dr Yusuf Dadoo, a leader of both the Transvaal Indian Congress and the CPSA, and timed to coincide in May 1948 with the whites-only general election. This issue was the cause of an unusually sharp clash between Mandela and Tambo, on the one hand, and Sisulu, on the other – he had been persuaded of the wisdom of the campaign. In an interview with Luli Callinicos in 1993, Mandela recalled that Ismail Meer and other members of the Transvaal Indian Congress, including Maulvi Cachalia, had been able to put forward persuasive and, he thought in retrospect, progressive arguments. 'Whereas Oliver and I were keeping in mind the mandate that was given to us by our executive, we were so annoyed with Comrade Walter as we walked down … Market Street – this meeting was almost just at the corner of Market and Diagonal streets, and we had to walk from there to Park Station to catch the train to Orlando – we left him behind and wouldn't talk to him at all!'

Sisulu later complained that Mandela and Tambo had used 'absolutely wrong methods'. They had not sought to persuade him back to the executive's position, but had tried to isolate him – they did not speak to each other for a couple of days. When the president of the Transvaal ANC, Constantine Ramahanoe, went against his own executive's decision and issued a statement in support of the campaign, Sisulu joined Mandela and Tambo in an attempt to censure him. The meeting of the executive broke up in disarray, but they had, in any case, failed to prevent participation by many members of the ANC in the campaign.

Mandela, in his memoir *The long walk to freedom*,

vividly recalled Tambo's surprisingly sanguine response to the National Party's victory in the 1948 elections. 'The victory was a shock … On election day, I attended a meeting with Oliver Tambo and some others. We barely discussed the question of a Nationalist government because we did not expect one. The meeting went on all night, and we emerged at dawn and found a newspaper vendor selling the *Rand Daily Mail*: the Nationalists had triumphed. I was stunned and dismayed, but Oliver took a more considered line. "I like this," he said. "I like this." I could not imagine why. He explained, "Now we will know exactly who our enemies are and where we stand."'

The radical racism of Dr D.F. Malan and the National Party government, which immediately began to implement the policies that came to be known as apartheid, prompted a radical response. By the end of 1948, the leaders of the Youth League, Mda, Sisulu, Mandela and Tambo, had drafted the Programme of Action. This restated a commitment to African nationalism and made provision for the use by the ANC for the first time of boycotts, strikes, civil disobedience and non-cooperation as a means of bringing about political change. The programme was discussed at the ANC conference in December 1948, but a decision on its adoption was postponed until the following year.

Tambo was, meanwhile, one of a group of ANC leaders, including Xuma, Sisulu and the communists Kotane and Marks, who rushed to Durban with Indian

Congress leaders, including Ismail Meer, to seek to quell the inter-communal riots that broke out there in January 1949. They also took part in a conference of African and Indian leaders, early in February, which produced a joint statement calling upon their people to seek ways of future cooperation.

In November 1949 Sisulu, Mandela and Tambo met Dr Xuma at his house in Sophiatown. They told him that he would only get the support of the Youth League in the election for the presidency at the forthcoming ANC conference if he backed the Programme of Action. He, reasonably in the circumstances, accused them of blackmail. He did not say that he opposed the programme, but he did say that he thought it was premature. He scoffed at his visitors' reference to the examples of Gandhi and Nehru, asking what they knew about these leaders, and he made it clear that he did not wish to go to prison as a martyr to their cause.

The meeting ended acrimoniously, with Xuma indicating that he did not need their support and throwing them out of the house. Tambo complained that he might at least have offered them transport home. All three of them were, however, later to show some remorse for the ruthless way in which they had treated the man who had been their patron and brought them into the ANC.

Professor Z.K. Matthews also made it clear that he thought the Programme of Action was too radical and declined their invitation to stand for the presidency. They then turned to Dr James Moroka, a wealthy Free State medical doctor and a landowner at Thaba Nchu, who had been a prominent member of the AAC, which had been set up in 1935 to fight Prime Minister Hertzog's 'Native Bills'. He was not, however, a paid-up member of the ANC, which he repeatedly referred to as the African National Council. With Youth League support, he defeated Xuma in the election for the post of president-general at the ANC conference in Bloemfontein in December 1949. Walter Sisulu was elected secretary-general and Tambo was elected to the NEC. Xuma had also been elected to the NEC, but soon resigned after publishing a letter – to the fury of Tambo – in which he implied that Moroka was a police informer.

Tambo may have established good relationships with individual communists, but his reservations about the CPSA persisted. As late as March 1950, when acting as president of the Transvaal branch of the ANC Youth League, he argued that Africa was not immune to the pressures of the Cold War. Communism would play a part in a new scramble for Africa, which should not catch Africa unawares: 'We must be vigilant and active lest we be swallowed up by foreign invaders.' He played a leading role at this time in breaking up a meeting of the Transvaal ANC in Springs when he realised that, if elections went ahead, communist candidates would win control of the province.

In an interview with Luli Callinicos, Godfrey Pitje, then also an articled clerk, who had been a lecturer and leader of the Youth League at Fort Hare, recalled that Tambo had said: 'The communists want to capture the leadership of the ANC and we dare not allow it.' Asked what they could do to stop the election of communists to the executive, Tambo said: 'You scream. You do anything that will make the comrades not to be elected.' Pitje recalled: 'So we screamed and shouted, and jumped on tables – and we succeeded in breaking up the conference, so no elections were held.'

Continuing tension between the Youth League and the ANC itself was demonstrated at this time by the former's attitude to the 'Defend Free Speech Convention', which was organised in the same month by the Transvaal ANC, the Transvaal Indian Congress, the African People's Organisation (APO, a coloured group), and the district committee of the Communist Party, to protest against the banning of Sam Kahn, a communist MP who represented 'Natives' in the Western Cape. Without consulting his executive, Dr Moroka had agreed to preside over the convention, which was a great success – it was attended by ten thousand people in Johannesburg's Market Square. It agreed to the calling of a May Day strike to demand the abolition of the pass laws and the repeal of all discriminatory legislation.

Mandela, Tambo and the Youth League objected to Moroka's involvement in the convention, as well as to the action of Walter Sisulu, who, as secretary-general, had sent a message of support. They also opposed the strike, seeing it as a CPSA event, and in competition with a day of protest that they were planning in terms of the Programme of Action. They did their best to frustrate the strike by heckling and breaking up pre-strike meetings, but they failed to stop it. Tragically, the police killed nineteen people and injured thirty more in clashes with demonstrators on May Day.

The government had already introduced a bill that was later passed as the Suppression of Communism Act, and the CPSA's central committee had voted that the party should dissolve itself on the day that the Act came into force. Sisulu, who had been quick to see there was a need for cooperation with other racial groups, realised that this legislation was also a threat to the ANC. Mandela and Tambo had not been so quick to appreciate this threat, but they now reluctantly dropped their opposition to cooperation with other groups. Sisulu invited representatives of the South African Indian Congress, the CPSA, the APO, the AAC and the Transvaal Council of Non-European Trade Unions, as well as the Youth League as a separate organisation, to a conference on 14 May to plan a response to the earlier tragedy. All of the organisations, with the single exception of the AAC, attended the meeting, which agreed to plan a day of mourning for those killed on May Day and of protest against the Suppression of Communism Act on 26 June.

The stay-away was only a partial success in Johannesburg and Durban, but it was highly successful in Port Elizabeth. Mandela later acknowledged that he had not been unsympathetic to the banning of the CPSA. He recalled, however, that he had, at the planning meeting for the June stay-away, heard Oliver Tambo utter prophetic words, which may have been inspired by those of Pastor Niemöller in the context of Nazi Germany: 'Today it is the Communist Party. Tomorrow it will be our trade unions, our Indian Congress, our APO, our African National Congress.'

Rusty Bernstein, in his memoir, *Memory against forgetting*, noted that it was at this planning meeting that 'Hatchets were buried including that between the Youth League and those who had convened the stay-at-home. A unified council of war was set up to run a joint campaign – something the movement had previously been unable to do. The government had created the first all-inclusive alliance against its own policies. There is little reference to that meeting in the histories, yet there – unnoticed – the foundation stone was laid for the ANC coalition that would come to dominate the next decades of South African liberation politics.'

Joe Slovo, in his unfinished memoir, recalled that 26 June had seen 'the first-ever national political general strike by black workers' in South Africa. The Suppression of Communism Act and the banning of the CPSA proved to be the catalyst for the emergence of a multiracial alliance on the basis of separate congresses for each of the racial groups.

3

From the Defiance Campaign to Sharpeville, 1951–60

Messrs Mandela and Tambo

Although increasingly active politically, Oliver Tambo continued to teach at St Peter's until May 1948. He was then able, with the help of Walter Sisulu, to secure a position as an articled clerk in a firm of attorneys which did Sisulu's conveyancing. Tambo had to leave St Peter's, where he had lived for five years, and moved to Wattville, Benoni, where he lived with his sister and her husband. Because he had a university degree, he was able to do his articles in three years, writing his legal exams by correspondence through the University of South Africa. He qualified in July 1951 and entered into a legal partnership with Nelson Mandela in the following year.

Ralph Tuch, who was only twenty-three when Tambo

joined the firm Kramer and Tuch, later Kowalsky and Tuch, had vivid memories of the somewhat older articled clerk. He described him as 'modest, moderate, softly spoken; a gentle person'. He recalled that one of the first cases in which Tambo played a leading role related to the land rights of the Bafokeng in the Rustenburg district – a group that would eventually become very wealthy through their ownership of mining rights. Tuch recalled: 'Whatever he did he would prepare well. He had a good legal brain … He could debate.' Tambo 'impressed people simply by his quiet way and approach … with arguments well presented. He always kept his cool …'

Writing in the introduction to Nelson Mandela's *No easy walk to freedom* (1966), Tambo gave his own account of the Mandela and Tambo partnership, which operated illegally from offices on the first floor of Chancellor House, Fox Street, opposite the Johannesburg Magistrate's Court: 'For years we worked side by side in the offices near the Courts. To reach our desks each morning, Nelson and I ran the gauntlet of patient queues of people overflowing from the chairs in the waiting-room into the corridors. South Africa has the dubious reputation of boasting one of the highest prison populations in the world. Jails are jam-packed with Africans imprisoned for serious offences – and crimes of violence are ever on the increase in apartheid society – but also for petty infringements of statutory law that no really civilised society would punish with imprisonment. To be unemployed is a crime because no African can for long evade arrest if his passbook does not carry the stamp of authorised and approved employment. To be landless can be a crime, and we interviewed weekly the delegations of grizzled, weather-worn peasants from the countryside, who came to tell us how many generations of their families had worked a little piece of land from which they were now being ejected. To brew African beer, to drink it or to use the proceeds to supplement the meagre family income is a crime, and women who do so face heavy fines and jail terms. To cheek a white man can be a crime. To live in the "wrong" area – an area declared white or Indian or Coloured – can be a crime for Africans. South African apartheid laws turn innumerable innocent people into "criminals". Apartheid stirs hatred and frustration among people. Young people, who should be in school or learning a trade, roam the streets, join gangs and wreak their revenge on the society that confronts them with only the dead-end alley of crime or poverty.

'Our buff office files carried thousands of these stories and if, when we started our law partnership, we had not been rebels against South African apartheid, our experiences in our offices would have remedied the deficiency. We had risen to professional status in our community, but every case in court, every visit to the prisons to interview clients, reminded us of the humiliation and suffering burning into our people.'

George Bizos noted that the sign in the first-floor

window reading 'Mandela & Tambo – Attorneys', painted in large letters and in the black, green and gold colours of the ANC, was thought by some to fall foul of the legal profession's ban on advertising. Many observers contrasted Mandela's flamboyant courtroom style with Tambo's restrained approach, but there was also agreement that they were both good lawyers. Ruth Mompati, who worked in the office for many years as Mandela's secretary, and who also worked very closely with Tambo for many years in exile in Zambia, recalled: 'Oliver was quiet. He was a reserved person, but he was a very strong person … And when he went to court, he dealt with cases as a man who had confidence. As a man who knew what he was doing.'

The Defiance Campaign

The formation of this partnership between two of the most prominent young leaders of the ANC seems to have coincided, more or less, with the launching of the Defiance Campaign on 26 June 1952, the second anniversary of the 'Day of Mourning and Protest'. The proliferation of apartheid legislation, and the forthcoming celebration in 1952 of the tercentenary of the arrival at the Cape of Jan van Riebeeck, demanded a political response. It was on 17 June 1951, the day of the funeral of Dr Pixley Seme, a founder of the ANC, that a meeting of the NEC approved the outline of what was to become the Defiance Campaign and agreed that there should be cooperation with the Indian Congress. A joint committee of the two congresses produced a blueprint, which was then approved by all the provinces, with the single exception of Natal, where the leadership was divided.

At the ANC conference in Bloemfontein in December 1951, Walter Sisulu, as secretary-general, announced the plans for a campaign of civil disobedience against 'unjust laws'. It was decided that Dr Moroka and Sisulu would write a joint letter to the prime minister, Dr Malan, to demand the repeal of six 'unjust laws', including the pass laws, the Group Areas Act, the Separate Representation of Voters Act, which sought to remove coloured men from the common voters' roll in the Cape, the Suppression of Communism Act, and the Bantu Authorities Act. If he refused to do so, the ANC would launch a Defiance Campaign. After the government's predictable rejection of these demands, the NEC met on 31 May and announced that the campaign would go ahead, as planned, on 26 June 1952.

Oliver Tambo was present with other leaders of the ANC and some leaders of the South African Indian Congress when the announcement was made at a banquet in Port Elizabeth. He was active in the organisation of the campaign, and spoke at public meetings in both Port Elizabeth and Durban, but, unlike Sisulu and Mandela, who became 'Volunteer Number 1', he was not among the eight thousand people who were arrested between June and December for defying unjust laws. Nor was he among the leaders of the two congresses who were arrested and charged in December in connection with organisation of the campaign. He had, as the result of a tactical decision, kept a relatively low profile, acting as secretary-general when Sisulu was in detention, and running the legal practice on his own while Mandela was detained. The Defiance Campaign generated work for the practice and Tambo spent a great deal of time in court.

There were two occasions during the campaign when Tambo made a conspicuous intervention. He was sent to Port Elizabeth as a troubleshooter when the success of the campaign there was endangered by riots, deaths by police action, a strike, and subsequent divisions within the ANC. Thomas Nkobi recalled that Tambo presided over an all-night meeting in KwaZakhele township, which resolved the crisis in the community.

Many people also recalled the speech that he made to a meeting of white sympathisers in the Darragh Hall, at St Mary's Cathedral in Johannesburg, in November, in which he made a specific call for the establishment of a white congress-aligned organisation. Rusty Bernstein, a founder of the Congress of Democrats, recalled: 'Tambo's address was delivered with great eloquence and charm. He explained the aims of the Defiance Campaign, and the way the African, Indian and Coloured communities had responded to it. But where did white South Africans stand, especially those liberal and democratic white

South Africans who opposed apartheid? If they remained silent and uninvolved while a struggle was under way to end unjust laws, those engaged in the struggle might well interpret their silence as collusion with racism and injustice. Their antagonism to the state could turn into anger against the white community as a whole. The Congresses opposed all racism, including black racism against whites. But it could not fight it alone. The time had come for those who sincerely shared the Congress aim of ending apartheid to take up their share of the burden.'

Walter Sisulu, who was on the platform with Bram Fischer and Tambo, was impressed and recalled the impact of Tambo's speech: 'I have no way of describing it. You take a thing by the tail. And you expose it. OR, in his artistic way of speaking, created a tremendous impression. Not only to me, but to the people who were there. Because he has a way – you take a snake by the tail and you are exposing its head.'

In spite of his reservations about cooperation between different racially based political organisations, Tambo played at this time a significant part in the formation of what was to become the multiracial Congress Alliance.

As a result of highly repressive legislation, providing for lengthy terms of imprisonment and flogging for people who incited the breaking of apartheid laws, the Defiance Campaign came to an end in December 1952. At the annual conference in that month there was also a change in the leadership. Dr Moroka, who had separated his own defence from that of other leaders of the ANC when on trial earlier in the month, and who had cut a somewhat pathetic figure in court, was replaced as president-general by Chief Albert Luthuli. The latter had impressed the membership by his strong leadership of the Defiance Campaign in Natal and had been stripped of his chieftaincy by the government.

The Congress of the People and the Freedom Charter

The Defiance Campaign had done a great deal to raise the profile and increase the membership of the ANC. Its conclusion left a gap that was only gradually filled with the move to a new campaign. Professor Z.K. Matthews had first proposed a Congress of the People to draw up a Freedom Charter at a meeting of the Cape ANC at Cradock in 1953. At the request of Chief Luthuli, he produced a memorandum on the subject and revived the proposal at a meeting at Stanger early in the following year. This meeting brought together forty delegates from the ANC, the South African Indian Congress, the Congress of Democrats, the newly formed Coloured People's Congress, and representatives of ANC-aligned trade unions, which were to form the South African Congress of Trade Unions (SACTU) in the following year. The meeting decided to go ahead with Matthews's proposal.

In his memorandum Matthews had written: 'Such

a Charter properly conceived as a mirror of the future South African Society can galvanise the people of South Africa into action and make them go over into the offensive against the reactionary forces at work in this country, instead of being perpetually on the defensive, fighting rearguard actions all the time.' Two years later, he was astonished to find that such 'innocent metaphorical expression' became the basis of the state's case in the Treason Trial when it was alleged that the memorandum had contemplated 'violent action of a military nature directed at the safety and independence of the State'.

Tambo became chairman of the working committee set up to organise the gathering of resolutions from the provinces, the drafting of the Freedom Charter, and the organisation of the Congress of the People. Rusty Bernstein, as a representative of the Congress of Democrats, worked closely with him and Walter Sisulu, and less closely with Mandela, over the following year. In his memoir, he provided illuminating character sketches of the men he saw as on their way to becoming the dominant triumvirate in the ANC. He saw Mandela as a charismatic leader, but Sisulu and Tambo as such different people that he found it hard to understand their evident closeness except in terms of 'their shared belief in the cause of liberation'. Sisulu was the wise counsellor, the deep strategic and tactical thinker, but he was always self-effacing and unassuming, achieving less recognition than he deserved. He travelled to the USSR and China in 1953 and joined the underground South African Communist Party (SACP) in 1955.

Of Tambo, and his experience of working with him in the planning of the Congress of the People, Bernstein wrote: 'We were miles apart ideologically. He was a devout and practising Christian who was finding himself, probably for the first time in his life, working in close harness with a white, non-ANC communist. I had the impression that he assumed that, as a communist, I had to have an agenda of my own. But he had great integrity and honesty. There were no occasions when he allowed his reservations about me or about communism to get in the way. He gave me and all my suggestions the same open and honest consideration as all others.

'Ideology never came between us. As we grew used to working together, his wariness towards me dissolved. We found ourselves in total agreement about almost everything all the time. I believe that he came to accept that my commitment was different from but no less than his own, though we started from different political premises. I developed a respect and admiration for him such as I have had for very few others, and which lasted till the end of his life.'

Bernstein may have overstated his role, but, by his own account, he was the primary draftsman and stylist of both the 'Call' to the Congress of the People and of the Freedom Charter itself. For the latter, he and a committee drew on thousands of suggestions that had been sent in from branches of the four congresses that made up the Congress Alliance. An essentially social democratic document, it became the guiding statement of the ANC both at home and in exile. Neither Tambo nor Bernstein was able to attend the Congress of the People in June 1955, which was attended by five thousand people. They were both banned from gatherings, but they got as close as they could to the Kliptown venue and watched from a distance. Mandela and Sisulu were also unable to attend, but were present on the fringe of the gathering.

Tambo had become acting secretary-general of the ANC in August 1954 when Walter Sisulu was issued with a banning order that compelled him to resign, at least nominally, from the ANC. Tambo was formally elected to the post in December 1955. He had himself received a banning order in 1954 that confined him to the magisterial districts of Johannesburg and Benoni and prohibited him from attending gatherings for two years, but he was able to carry on with his ANC and legal work. With Chief Luthuli immobilised in rural Natal by a banning order, Tambo played a leading role in the organisation of the Congress of the People, the campaign against the forced removal of black residents from Johannesburg's Western Areas (including Sophiatown) in terms of the Group Areas Act, and the implementation of the Bantu Education Act.

In terms of the latter Act, which was passed in 1953, the state was to take control of all mission schools in April 1955. Tambo was in the forefront of members of the NEC demanding an indefinite boycott of Bantu Education schools. Mandela and Sisulu thought that this was impractical and advocated a short-term boycott. In his report as secretary-general to the ANC's annual conference in December 1955, Tambo acknowledged that the long-term boycott strategy had failed as the ANC lacked the organisational capacity or the financial resources to make alternative provision. At the same time, he insisted that the fight against Bantu Education must go on: 'We must build steadily, carrying the people with us, exposing the wickedness of the new Bantu Education syllabus and the way the children are to be indoctrinated, achieving the boycott of the school boards and committees, adapting the form of protest to the state of preparedness in the area and the local conditions there.' He also acknowledged tactical errors in the campaign against the forced removals from Sophiatown. The government had been able to exploit the division between landlords and tenants, and it had been a mistake to suggest that non-violent resistance could actually stop the removals.

Tambo had worked closely with Father Trevor Huddleston in both these campaigns. It may have been through their combined influence that the Anglican Church decided to close St Peter's, Rosettenville, and all but one of its other African schools rather than hand them over to the state.

It was also through the Anglican Church that Tambo

began to acquire an international profile. Early in 1954, he met and greatly impressed Canon John Collins, from St Paul's Cathedral in London, who was on a two-month tour of South Africa. Collins recorded his impressions in his diary, describing Tambo as '[a] man of intelligence and dedication, without self-seeking and an exceptionally warm and attractive personality: a truly Christian spirit'. This meeting marked the beginning of a friendship and political alliance that were to be hugely important in the exile years.

Tambo's banning in August 1954 prompted Huddleston to write an article for the London *Observer*, which was published in October. He interviewed Tambo about his early life for this article, which brought Huddleston into direct conflict with his bishop and his community – a conflict that resulted in his withdrawal by the Community of the Resurrection from South Africa two years later. He recalled the circumstances in his bestselling memoir, *Naught for your comfort* (1956): 'it would be hard to find a more devoted churchman than Oliver Tambo. It was for this reason that when I heard that he had been banned in terms of the Suppression of Communism Act I took up my pen and wrote for the London *Observer* an article entitled "The Church Sleeps On". It seemed to me then and it seems to me now quite intolerable that the great mass of Christian people in South Africa should remain entirely unmoved when a man of Oliver's stature was victimised in this way. Of course it had already happened to many others, to trade unionists, to left-wing publicists, to almost every African and Indian leader of any stature. But here was, it seemed to me, a unique opportunity for the Church to protest and to demand to be heard on behalf of one of her most faithful sons. She did nothing.'

It was Huddleston's example that prompted Tambo, while still secretary-general of the ANC, to seek ordination in the Church of the Province of South Africa (the Anglican Church). He wept when he heard in 1956 of Huddleston's enforced withdrawal from the country, but he went on to apply to the newly appointed Bishop of Johannesburg, Ambrose Reeves, for ordination. His application was accepted, and he might have entered the church then if it had not been for his arrest, two weeks later on 21 December 1956, with 155 other political activists of all races and a variety of political persuasions, on a charge of high treason.

Courtship and marriage

Tambo first met his future wife, Adelaide Frances Tshukudu, at an ANC Youth League meeting in 1946, when he was twenty-nine and she was seventeen – and a pupil at Orlando High School. She had been radicalised at the age of ten by the brutal treatment of her beloved grandfather by the police. They corresponded for a while after their first meeting, but they did not get together until six or seven years later when he was in legal practice with

Mandela and she was completing her training as a nurse in Pretoria. Adelaide came from a Sotho-speaking family in Vereeniging, where her father and uncles worked in the local steel mill. She was born into a Methodist family, but became a Catholic at primary school. They shared strong political and religious convictions, but their path to marriage was not entirely smooth.

He proposed in 1954, but it took him two years to persuade her to accept his proposal. She had to overcome some resistance in her family to an inter-ethnic match – their membership of different churches was also a problem. Oliver was prepared to listen to the arguments of a priest, but he was not impressed by the Catholic Church's insistence that children of the marriage, as yet unborn, should be brought up as Catholics.

At the time of these negotiations, he intended to become an Anglican priest, and he must have been aware that his wife would be expected to support him in his pastoral role. In the end Adelaide concluded that her church was being unreasonable and she also came under pressure from members of her family who insisted that a woman should follow her husband in such matters. She agreed, somewhat reluctantly, that she should become an Anglican. There was also a problem when members of her family insisted on the payment of an unreasonably large sum of money as lobola, but they backed down when she threatened to get married at the registry office without it.

On 9 August 1956 Adelaide took part in the march

by twenty thousand women on the Union Buildings in Pretoria, which was organised by the Federation of South African Women in protest against the introduction of passes for African women. A marriage date was fixed for 22 December 1956 and then, on 5 December, there were the Treason Trial arrests. She received the news of Oliver's arrest at 6 a.m. on 6 December. The accused were not taken to court until 19 December and were only released on bail two days later – just in time for the wedding to go ahead in Benoni on the appointed day. There was a further mishap in the early hours of the wedding day when they were arrested with the best man, M.B. Yengwa, on the grounds that they did not have night passes. As a lawyer Tambo was exempt, but it took a call to counsel before they were released – with an unprecedented apology. The wedding went ahead without further accident. The newly married couple stayed for a while with Oliver's sister and her husband in Wattville, but they soon moved to their own house in the same location.

Some of their friends were surprised by this marriage alliance as Oliver and Adelaide seemed to have such strongly contrasting personalities, but they later concluded that they complemented each other. Oliver was usually described as low-key to the point of reticence, though capable of humour and assertiveness, but Adelaide was known for her dramatic dresses, hats and wigs, and was often described as flamboyant. In an obituary Paul Joseph, recalling her later years in London, described her as follows: 'She had a strong physical presence – reinforced by a variety of African headdresses and garments – a booming voice and laughed a lot. With her commanding personality, sometimes almost intimidating, she had an ability to get results ...'

The first child of the marriage, Thembi Gugulethu Nosinini, a daughter, was born on 19 October 1957. A son, Thabo Dalindlela, known as Dali, was born less than two years later on 1 March 1959. Their third child, and second daughter, Tselane, was born in London in 1962.

The Treason Trial and after

The Treason Trial disrupted Tambo's plans for marriage and ordination. The accused were flown from all corners of the country to Johannesburg, where they were held at the Fort for over two weeks before they were released on bail on 21 December. The preparatory examination began in January 1957 and the accused then appeared before a special court in Pretoria, where the case ran until September. The number of the accused was eventually reduced to thirty and the main trial ran for three years from 1958 to 1961, when all the remaining accused were acquitted. For reasons that remain obscure, Tambo, the secretary-general, and Luthuli, the president-general, were among the first to be dropped from the case in January 1957. Mandela and Sisulu remained on trial until 1961. By that time, Tambo himself had left the country and gone into exile.

As Sydney Kentridge, one of the junior counsel during the trial and later a leader of the Bar in Johannesburg and London, recalled: 'The prosecution's case was based on the allegation that the common objective of all the parties to the Congress movement (and of the ANC in particular) was to overthrow the state by violence'. Tambo had to carry the burden of running the ANC for much of the duration of the trial, as well as the task of liaison with the team of defence lawyers. It fell to him to brief Kentridge on the history of the ANC and its commitment to non-violence: 'Oliver ... took me through the history of the ANC and the development of its policies, from the Africans' Claims document of the mid-1940s to the Freedom Charter of 1955. He left me in no doubt of the genuineness of the ANC's policy of non-violence. It was a policy in which he believed deeply, and which the ANC maintained until circumstances after its banning in 1960 drove it into militancy. His own adherence, for as long as possible, to the doctrine of non-violent resistance seemed to me to spring both from his deep Christian faith and from a hard-headed practical assessment of the forces of the apartheid government and the ruthlessness of that government.'

One of the major goals of the prosecution was to associate the ANC with communism, and Tambo made his own position clear to Kentridge: 'Marxism had no attraction for Oliver but his viewpoint was that the ANC was not merely a political party, it was a national movement that accommodated communists, socialists, nationalists, believers in God and atheists, provided only that they were committed to the fundamental objective of the ANC – a non-racial, egalitarian, democratic South Africa.'

The involvement of both Tambo and Mandela as defendants in the first year of the Treason Trial had a damaging impact on their legal practice. When Tambo was released from the case at the end of 1957, he found that the firm owed £1,000 to advocates and was on the verge of bankruptcy. Much of this debt related to the trial, and Tambo asked Bishop Ambrose Reeves and the Treason Trial Defence Fund for a loan that would be repaid over ten months. Reeves passed the request on to Canon Collins in London, who was able to find the money in a contingency fund. Although released from the trial, Tambo found it difficult because of banning orders to practise his profession. He was unable to act on behalf of people who were accused in connection with the Sekhukhuneland Revolt, and he was deported from South West Africa when he flew to Windhoek in December 1959 to act on behalf of Sam Nujoma and other nationalists.

It is, perhaps, surprising that while on trial in 1957 Tambo was able to supervise a new and more comprehensive constitution for the ANC, often known as the 'Tambo constitution', which was, like its 1943 predecessor, not specific about African membership. It created the post of deputy president, to which Tambo was himself elected in 1958.

The 'Africanists'

The opening statement of the Freedom Charter – 'South Africa belongs to all who live in it' – proved to be its most contentious clause, prompting an 'Africanist' backlash at the annual conference in December 1955, and causing intermittent argument until the final rupture in the Transvaal ANC in November 1958. As founders of the Youth League, Tambo, Mandela and Sisulu had all been 'Africanists' once. Sisulu was probably the first of this triumvirate to recognise the need for multiracial alliances. Ironically, many participants noticed that it was the Treason Trial, which brought leading members of the four congresses together day after day for most of a year in the Johannesburg Drill Hall, and a smaller number for a longer period later on in Pretoria, that really cemented the Congress Alliance. Tambo had made his own personal contribution to group solidarity, among the men anyway, as conductor of the 'Accused Male Voices Choir'.

Among the 'Africanists' were several people, including A.P. Mda and Peter Raboroko, who had been among the founders of the Youth League. Their rising star was Robert Sobukwe, a lecturer in African languages at Wits University, who had been a leader of the Youth League at Fort Hare in 1948–9, though he had not subsequently been politically active. Their campaign against the leadership of the ANC and the 'multiracial' Congress Alliance, which was led by Potlako Leballo and the Orlando branch and by Josias Madzunya in Alexandra, reached its climax in early November 1958 at the conference of the Transvaal ANC.

In his opening address, Chief Albert Luthuli spoke of 'a dangerously narrow African nationalism' and a reversion to tribalism. The 'Africanists', some of them carrying sticks, constituted a rowdy block in the hall and were, allegedly, prepared to use violence in their bid to take control of the ANC in the province. Tambo chaired the meeting and insisted that only delegates who were accepted by the credentials committee would be allowed to vote in elections. When he adjourned the meeting late at night on 1 November, he indicated that the elections would be held according to the rules on the following day.

Overnight, Robert Resha assembled a group of ANC 'volunteers', armed with sticks and iron bars, who gathered behind the hall and who were also, allegedly, prepared to back up Tambo's 'delegates only' ruling with force if necessary. The 'Africanists', some of them similarly armed, assembled at the front of the hall, which was locked, with Tambo standing at the door. Seeing that they were outnumbered and had no chance of winning in the elections, they withdrew from the meeting, and then from the ANC itself. In a letter they sent into the meeting, written by Sobukwe but signed by another person, they denied that they were a 'paramilitary clique' or that they were ready to resort to violence. They rejected the 'Kliptown Charter' as in conflict with the earlier Programme of Action and claimed that they were 'the custodians of the ANC policy as it was formulated in 1912'. The time had come, they said, for 'a parting of the ways'.

Benjamin Pogrund, then a young journalist writing for the liberal weekly *Contact*, and later the author of an enthusiastic biography of Sobukwe, had been advised to leave the meeting in the interests of his own safety, but he wrote an account of it on the basis of interviews. There is no evidence that there was actual, as opposed to potential, violence on the second day of the meeting, but Pogrund asserted that 'strong-arm men had beaten the heads of dissidents'. In a later memoir he said that he had shown the draft of his article to Tambo, who expressed surprise and exclaimed: 'This did not happen. What is this?' According to Pogrund, he held his ground and after a few minutes 'Tambo dropped his innocent front'. This was, Pogrund maintained, an example of something that he saw quite often. Tambo 'had a reserved, deceptive air about him that concealed a nimble mind and a talent for political maneuvering. These characteristics were to stand him in good stead during the thirty years he later spent in exile and keeping the ANC alive and strong.'

Tambo took a different view of what had happened. Some years later, he noted that the Africanists' plans to railroad the conference had failed because 'for as long as was procedurally possible, they were allowed all the rights and privileges of accredited delegates and enjoyed the full protection of the chairman', but when 'the critical moment came when the chairman had to order that they be forcibly taken out [and] the moment of violence for which they had prepared' was about to become a reality, their nerve failed. The truth seems to be that the 'Africanists' were not only outnumbered, but also outmanoeuvred.

In his annual report as secretary-general in December 1958, six weeks after the Transvaal conference, Tambo wrote: 'The government, the Africanists, and other enemies of the A.N.C., including the hostile press, joined hands and formed a hostile front against the Congress movement. They all claimed that the A.N.C. was preparing to establish a communist state on the basis of the Freedom Charter, that the A.N.C. was controlled and directed by the C.O.D. [Congress of Democrats], that the alliance of the Congress Movement was detrimental to the true interest of the African people. The Africanists set themselves the task of breaking the special conference of the A.N.C. Transvaal, if necessary by force. When they realised that the efforts to break the Conference had failed because of the effective counter measures taken by the Organisation, they suddenly announced their secession. We welcome their departure from our organisation.'

After their withdrawal from the ANC, the 'Africanists' went on to establish the Pan Africanist Congress under the leadership of Robert Sobukwe, with Potlako Leballo as national secretary, at a meeting in April 1959. In his opening speech Sobukwe made an eloquent plea for pan-Africanism and African unity. He rejected the idea that the word 'race' could be used in the plural – there was only one race, the human race. He insisted that 'multi-racialism [is] a pandering to European bigotry and arrogance' and a method of safeguarding white interests – it was 'racialism multiplied'. The core of his speech was the statement 'We aim, politically, at government of the Africans by the Africans, for the Africans, with everybody who owes his only loyalty to Afrika and who is prepared to accept the democratic rule of an African majority being regarded as an African. We guarantee no minority rights, because we think in terms of individuals, not groups.'

The ANC secretary-general's report in December 1959, signed by Tambo's successor, Duma Nokwe, made it clear that there was no question of the ANC abandoning its role as the leader of the African people. The report made it clear, however, that the ANC's legal existence was under threat: 'Not only has the government banned practically every senior leader of our organisation, banned our organisation in some parts of the country [such as Sekhukhuneland], prohibited in almost all proclaimed areas all public gatherings of a political nature, but it is also constantly making statements threatening to ban the whole organisation.'

Tambo had been told by Chief Luthuli in April 1958

that, in the event of the banning of the ANC as a whole, the NEC had decided that he should be sent abroad as its roving ambassador. Adelaide Tambo expressed reluctance to leave elderly members of their families. For Oliver, it would mean abandoning his calling to enter the church, but he said then: 'We can't say no to the organisation.' In the end circumstances permitted a delay of two years. In December 1958 the ANC set up an Anti-Pass Council and an Economic Boycott Committee. These jointly planned a year-long campaign of selective boycotts of consumer goods and of protests, which would be launched on 26 June 1959, and reach a climax in May–June 1960. Anti-pass demonstrations were brought forward to 31 March 1960, but the PAC then stole a march on the ANC by announcing its own anti-pass demonstration for 21 March and inviting the ANC to take part. An unintended consequence of this pre-emptive move was the Sharpeville Massacre, in which sixty-nine men, women and children were killed. A state of emergency was declared and the ANC and PAC were banned shortly afterwards. It is hardly surprising that Tambo's retrospective account of this event showed unusual signs of bitterness. 'With typical disregard for united action, the PAC had earlier sent and published a letter "inviting" the ANC to abandon the massive countrywide plans for action, and to join at very short notice an unplanned, hurried switch … to an ill-prepared campaign, which, but for the police bullets at Sharpeville, was doomed to fail …'

This action by the 'Africanists' was the immediate cause of Tambo's departure from South Africa, followed soon afterwards by that of his wife and two young children, into more than thirty years of exile. He left the country and crossed the border into the Bechuanaland Protectorate in the early hours of 31 March 1960.

4

Into exile: London and Tanzania, 1960–67

The Sharpeville Massacre was the immediate cause of Tambo's leaving South Africa, but he and Walter Sisulu had been making contingency plans for his departure for some time. They had both, together with Yusuf Cachalia of the Transvaal Indian Congress, interviewed Frene Ginwala, who was working with the congress. She had just returned from the United Kingdom, where she had been studying law, and had contacts in East Africa. She suggested that Julius Nyerere, leader of the Tanganyika African National Union (TANU) in Tanganyika, which was soon to become self-governing, was sympathetic to the South African cause, and would be able to facilitate the transit of an ANC leader through the country.

Sisulu asked her to travel to Salisbury in Southern Rhodesia and to coordinate Tambo's journey from there.

She was also asked to contact TANU and the Indian government to secure passports. She left Johannesburg for Mozambique, where her parents were traders, on 22 March, the day after Sharpeville, and was in Salisbury a few days later. She was looked after there by the historian Terence Ranger and his wife, Shelagh – they were the local contacts of Canon Collins and Christian Action, which funded Tambo's flight.

Tambo met Ronald Segal, a young member of the Congress of Democrats, in Cape Town on 29 March, and they agreed to leave for Bechuanaland that evening using his mother's car. Segal had been involved in the boycott campaign and had embarrassed Tambo at a meeting in the previous year by publicly demanding membership of the ANC and brandishing a pound note, but they had since then established a good relationship. They passed through Johannesburg on the following day and Tambo was able to say goodbye to Adelaide and the children – she had just returned from visiting Sharpeville, where she had family. They went together to see a lawyer, possibly George Bizos, to get Adelaide a power of attorney, and then went to tell Bishop Ambrose Reeves that Oliver was leaving the country.

Tambo and Segal left Johannesburg late at night and crossed the unguarded Bechuanaland border without passports, reaching the small town of Lobatse in the early hours of Sunday, 31 March. Meanwhile, in South Africa, the leaders of the Congress Alliance were being rounded up and a state of emergency was declared. The ANC and PAC were formally banned on 8 April, by which time the entire leadership of the Congress Alliance had been detained. Segal returned immediately to Johannesburg, where he learned of the round-up of activists and the success of that day's stay-away in protest against Sharpeville.

Concluding, after some agonising, that he was at risk of detention and would be more useful with Tambo, he returned to Bechuanaland on the following day, 2 April. They had the support there of Seretse Khama, a traditional leader who was about to enter politics, and a few liberal members of the colonial administration. They were allowed freedom of movement, though they were under South African surveillance, and there were rumours of kidnap and assassination plots. By 9 April they had reached Francistown where, Segal recalled, they heard the news of David Pratt's unsuccessful attempt to assassinate the prime minister, Dr Verwoerd. There they met Dr Yusuf Dadoo, former leader of the South African Indian Congress and a current leader of the underground SACP, who had left South Africa soon after Tambo on a similar mission.

Segal's elder brother drove down from Salisbury to warn them not to travel overland through Southern Rhodesia. If they did so, they would be arrested and returned to South Africa. The authorities told them that they would not be allowed to use the airstrip at

Francistown, which belonged to the South African mines' recruitment agency, WENELA, so they moved to Palapye and eventually flew out from there to Nyasaland (present-day Malawi) in a chartered plane. It had flown in from Salisbury, and brought them blank Indian passports, which Ginwala had obtained from Kenya. She flew on ahead to Tanganyika, by way of Blantyre, Nyasaland, preparing the way for Tambo, Segal and Dadoo in both places.

Phil Howard, the local manager of the British trading company Booker Brothers, McConnell, met them at the airport and they spent the night with him and his Anglo-Indian wife. The Howards introduced them to representatives of the Nyasaland Congress Party, including the youthful Aleke Banda and three clergymen, including the Reverend Andrew Ross, a young Scottish missionary. The chief magistrate rejected a South African attempt to extradite them, arguing that they could only be returned to Bechuanaland. Their Indian passports were confiscated, but they flew on to Tanganyika early the next morning without them.

Frene Ginwala met them at Dar es Salaam airport and took them to meet Julius Nyerere, who had cleared their safe transit with the Governor, Sir Richard Turnbull. Tambo flew on after a few days via Nairobi, where he was given another Indian passport, and Rome to Tunisia, using a ticket that David Wirmark, the Swedish president of the World Assembly of Youth had sent to him through

Seretse Khama. Wirmark had invited Tambo to speak at the first Pan African Youth Seminar and recalled that he 'gave a fantastic speech about the struggle for freedom in South Africa. It was on the basis of non-violence, which was the policy of the ANC at the time.'

This was the first speech that Tambo ever gave on behalf of the ANC outside South Africa – the first of thousands that he was to give over thirty years. While in Tunis, Tambo met President Habib Bourguiba and the Ghanaian ambassador, who arranged for him to travel to Accra. Kwame Nkrumah, the Ghanaian prime minister, welcomed him warmly, but he had already met representatives of the PAC, with which he later sided. Tambo went on from Accra to Copenhagen via Dakar and Paris.

He was rushed from the airport to the stadium in Copenhagen where he addressed a May Day crowd of fifty thousand people. He told them that the best strategy against apartheid was a political and economic boycott. To people who said that an economic boycott would make the black people of South Africa poorer, his answer was that nothing could make them poorer than they were already. This was his first visit to one of the Nordic countries, which were eventually, but not immediately, to become major financial backers of the ANC. At the end of the day he told his host that it had been 'a very long, but wonderful first day of my life in Europe'.

London

By the time Tambo reached London, where he was to be based for four years, and where his family were to stay for over thirty years, he had passed through ten countries in the month since he left South Africa. He had never previously had a passport, and had set foot in only one country other than his own, but this was a harbinger of his future way of life. He was welcomed at London airport by his great friend Father Trevor Huddleston, then serving in an inner-city London parish, but soon to become Bishop of Masasi in Tanganyika/Tanzania, where he remained until 1968.

Tambo was invited to stay by Canon John Collins and his wife, Diana, in their large house, 2 Amen Court, close to St Paul's Cathedral. They occupied the house by virtue of John's appointment as a canon of the cathedral through the patronage of the postwar Labour prime minister Clement Attlee. Collins was a gifted publicist, fundraiser and social entrepreneur who played a major role in the establishment of the Campaign for Nuclear Disarmament, Christian Action, the Anti-Apartheid Movement (AAM) and what became the International Defence and Aid Fund (IDAF). Tambo's membership of the Anglican Church and his alliances with Huddleston and Collins were to be immensely important to him and his family, as well as to the ANC as a whole, for most of the exile years. It was with good reason that Oliver described himself as Collins's 'eldest African son'.

Collins, through Christian Action and the IDAF, had not only financed Tambo's exit from South Africa, but also funded the travels of Adelaide and the three children, who arrived in London on 15 September after a long and complicated journey that took them to Swaziland, Bechuanaland and Ghana. The fund almost immediately began to pay the rent for a flat for the Tambos in Cholmeley Park, north London, and later paid the mortgage on the detached house at 51 Alexandra Park Road, Muswell Hill, which became their long-term family home. It also contributed in later years towards the children's fees at private boarding schools – expenses that could be justified in terms of the real threat posed by the apartheid regime to the family's security in London. These payments were not only subsidies to the family, but were also indirect contributions to the viability of the ANC itself. Adelaide Tambo went out to work as a nurse almost as soon as she arrived in London, often did two jobs, and worked very long hours.

There was no real ANC 'external mission' in Tambo's first few years in London. From June 1960 until January 1962, the ANC presence was subsumed within the South African United Front, which Tambo, under pressure from Ghana and the few other independent African states, had played the leading role in establishing. It linked the ANC, PAC, the South West Africa National Union (SWANU) and, briefly, the South West Africa People's Organisation

(SWAPO) in an uneasy alliance, with nominally joint representation in London, New York, Cairo, Accra and Dar es Salaam. The front collapsed early in 1962 when it was found that the PAC in Ghana was actively campaigning against the ANC.

In his first few years in London, Tambo tried hard to get recognition and support from the British government. As Adelaide Tambo told Anthony Sampson, he waited endlessly for interviews with the Foreign and Commonwealth Office – 'he never stopped knocking'. He made no headway with a government that suspected the ANC of communist sympathies, preferred the frankly anti-communist PAC, and was opposed to the trade boycott of South Africa, which the ANC advocated. One of the first diplomatic successes of the Anti-Apartheid Movement and the ANC in exile was the exclusion of South Africa from the Commonwealth – a move that was opposed by the government of Harold Macmillan. Although the government allowed Tambo and other exiles to settle in London, it provided no recognition or support. Its hostility was only increased by the turn to armed struggle, which became public knowledge in 1962–3, and by the ANC's enforced turn to the USSR for military and financial assistance in 1963. Tambo had to wait twenty-six years after his arrival in London before he received an invitation to cross the threshold of the Foreign Office.

Tambo was able to make good contacts in the Scandinavian countries from 1960 onwards, travelling to Sweden for the first time in 1961, and again in 1962 when he met the prime minister, Tage Erlander, and first made contact with the future prime minister Olof Palme, then a junior official. In the course of the 1960s he established a good relationship with both the Swedish Liberal Party and the Social Democratic Party, but the ANC received no direct funding at all from Sweden until 1972, and no significant funding until after the Soweto Uprising in 1976, when Sweden became its most important cash donor. There was Scandinavian, as well as United Nations, funding for the Defence and Aid Fund, which was vital for the Rivonia Trial defence in 1963–4 and for the long-term support of prisoners' families, but little of that reached the ANC itself. The Anti-Apartheid Movement was always short of cash and was not a source of funds for the ANC.

Armed struggle

Tambo was not personally involved in the debates about the turn to armed struggle, or sabotage, which went on within the ANC in 1960–1 and led to the formation of Umkhonto we Sizwe (MK) as a nominally autonomous armed wing in July 1961. He was not fully briefed about the decision when, in the later months of 1961, he participated in the campaign for the award of the Nobel Peace Prize to Chief Luthuli. He accompanied Luthuli and his wife to Oslo for the award ceremony on 10 December 1961. The first MK campaign was launched within a week – on 16 December.

According to Joe Matthews, a well-informed source, Tambo was shocked by the move to armed struggle, which had been initially opposed by Luthuli and Moses Kotane among others, as well as by the South African Indian Congress. Joe Matthews recalled: 'Tambo was very upset by the decision to embark on armed struggle because he started off in 1960 abroad and the organisation was still on the non-violent struggle. The South African United Front which he had established … was based of course on non-violence. He accompanied Chief Luthuli to receive the Nobel Peace Prize. So to get this news of armed struggle and violent struggle … was totally contradictory to what he had been preaching abroad … And I think he actually wrote a letter … to the leadership inside the country … questioning this approach … It's only when Mandela toured and met Tambo outside the country that … the strategy was eventually accepted by Tambo.'

The turn to armed struggle must certainly have embarrassed Tambo, who had, in his first two years in exile, made many speeches emphasising the commitment to non-violence of the Congress Alliance and advocating trade sanctions as an alternative to armed struggle. Luthuli's speech in Oslo, which he helped to write, emphasised the non-violent nature of the movement towards independence in Africa as a whole, was Christian in tone, and made no reference to communism.

This change of tack was also embarrassing to Canon Collins and Christian Action, as its backers included many Quakers and other pacifists. Tambo and Collins were, of course, able to produce arguments to justify the turn to violence in terms of Christian theories of 'just war'. Speaking many years later, in 1980, to the World Council of Churches, for example, Tambo said: 'When those who worship Christ shall have, in pursuit of just peace, taken up arms against those who hold the majority in subjection by force of arms, then shall it truly be said of such worshippers also: "Blessed are the peacemakers for they also shall be called the sons of God."'

Mandela, travelling with Joe Matthews, left South Africa on his clandestine journey to Africa and Europe early in January 1962, travelling, as Tambo had done two years previously, by way of Bechuanaland and Tanganyika. He met Tambo in Nigeria late in January and they then travelled together to Addis Ababa for the conference of PAFMECSA (the Pan African Freedom Movement for East, Central and Southern Africa). They represented the ANC as joint leaders at the conference – Tambo was elected to the PAFMECSA executive. In his speech to the conference Mandela did not explicitly acknowledge the link between the ANC and MK. Although this soon became widely known, Tambo did not publicly acknowledge it until after the conclusion of the Rivonia Trial in July 1964.

Tambo only received his first full briefings from

Mandela about MK in Lagos in January 1962 and at their later meetings in Addis Ababa, Accra and London. There is a suggestion in Mandela's later report to the NEC that Tambo had been deliberately kept out of the loop about a proposed military training camp in Tanganyika, which would have been a joint venture of the ANC and the SACP. Mandela noted that Tambo had been puzzled about this and that Frene Ginwala knew more about it than he did. Nyerere suggested that the ANC should postpone the launch of armed struggle and that Ethiopia could be a possible base for future training. It was not until 1964 that he allowed the ANC to open a camp at Kongwa for people who had returned from military training elsewhere.

Tambo participated with Mandela in London in various meetings with opposition leaders, including Hugh Gaitskell and Denis Healey of the Labour Party and Jo Grimond, leader of the Liberal Party, but there was no contact with Conservative MPs or the government. They also met David Astor, editor of the *Observer* and a financial backer of the Africa Bureau, which was a pressure group associated with the Reverend Michael Scott, a clerical rival of Collins in the anti-apartheid field. the *Observer*'s coverage of the Rivonia Trial in 1963–4 was later to be highly influential.

Mandela was arrested within weeks of his return to South Africa and the internal ANC was plunged into crisis. Tambo presided over a meeting of external representatives in Dar es Salaam in August, which was attended by Tennyson Makiwane, Robert Resha, Raymond Mazisi Kunene and J.J. Hadebe, among others. The last meeting between members of what was coming to be known as the 'external mission' and people from inside South Africa took place at Lobatse in Bechuanaland in October 1962. The external delegation consisted of Tambo, Mzwai Piliso, Moses Mabhida and Tennyson Makiwane, together with Joe Matthews, who flew in from Basutoland and liaised with the Protectorate government of Bechuanaland. The delegates from inside South Africa included Govan Mbeki, who chaired the meeting, Walter Sisulu, Dan Tloome and Moses Kotane. This conference, which was closely monitored by British intelligence, apparently agreed to suspend the ANC's constitution for the duration, and recognised Tambo's position as the leader of the ANC in exile.

Wilton Mkwayi found on his return from China to London in August 1962 that Tambo was then unaware that he, with others, including Joe Gqabi, had been sent there for military training. Mkwayi also recalled that Tambo had difficulty getting a visa for Tanzania at that time, and suggested that Tennyson Makiwane and Robert Resha were trying to keep him out of Africa, which they saw as their preserve. According to Mkwayi, Tambo was told at Lobatse in October that he had been kept in the dark about the military plans because his position in London could be compromised if it was known that he was involved in the armed struggle. Mkwayi recalled: 'He was such a magnanimous and understanding person that on his return from Botswana, he told me that those responsible for organising the trip to China profusely apologised to him for not following correct procedures. They explained to him that they were going to maintain the official ANC policy, which maintained that the military wing was subordinate to the political wing.'

The question of the terms of the relationship between the political and the military wings of the ANC was one that was to keep on recurring. There may have been a link between Tambo's reservations about armed struggle and his being sidelined at this time. It is also possible that the central committee of the SACP had organised military training in China without reference to the ANC as a whole. Mkwayi thought that the attitude towards Tambo that was displayed at this time by Tennyson Makiwane, his elder brother/cousin Ambrose Makiwane, and Alfred Kgokong (Themba Mqota) foreshadowed the open conflict with them that erupted following the Morogoro Conference in 1969 and resulted in their eventual expulsion in 1975 as members of the so-called Gang of Eight.

Tambo clearly had some difficulty in establishing his overall leadership of the ANC in exile, and there was also a continuing question mark over the leadership of MK. After the Rivonia Trial and the virtual elimination of the internal leadership, he emerged as the de facto leader and major spokesperson of the ANC, but he did not become acting president until the death of Luthuli in 1967, and was not recognised as substantive president until 1977.

Funding

The most pressing problem facing Tambo and the ANC in exile was funding. Mandela had mentioned in his PAFMECSA report the serious financial difficulties that Tambo and the external mission faced. Promises of support amounting to about £40,000 were made by various countries at that conference, but it is not certain that they were all honoured. The establishment of the Organisation of African Unity (OAU) and its Liberation Committee in 1963 should have provided an important source of funding, but it proved to be disappointing.

Tambo visited Moscow for the first time while en route to Beijing in April 1963 and returned for a two-day visit in October. He returned there with the newly appointed MK commander, Joe Modise, in 1965. Funding from the USSR began in 1963 and ran until the early 1970s at the rate of about £100,000 a year with a significantly smaller contribution to the SACP. The USSR also began to provide military training and other logistical support from 1963 onwards, with several hundred trained men returning from there to Tanzania in 1964–5. The Soviet contribution in cash, though generous, probably amounted to less than half the budgetary requirements of the ANC in the mid-1960s and significantly less than half the larger budget (around $1 million) of the early 1970s. It is not clear how the shortfall was made up, though there were smaller contributions from some other countries in the Soviet bloc and from some African countries. Although the ANC tried to remain non-aligned in the early stages of the Sino-Soviet split, China soon sided with the PAC and ceased to be a source of funding or military training.

While based in London from 1960 to 1964, Tambo was always on the move and was never the chief representative of the ANC in the United Kingdom. This job was done in the early 1960s by Tennyson Makiwane, who arrived in 1959. He was succeeded by Robert Resha, and then by the poet Raymond Mazisi Kunene.

When the government of Tanzania allowed the ANC to open a military camp in 1964, the 'provisional headquarters', which consisted of Tambo, Duma Nokwe, secretary-general, Alfred Kgokong, director of publicity, Moses Kotane, treasurer-general, and J.B. Marks, director of transport and communications, the last two both senior members of the SACP, moved from London to Dar es Salaam. As a result of Tanzanian government pressure, the headquarters moved again to Morogoro at the end of 1965. The smaller East African regional office remained in Dar es Salaam with Mzwai Piliso as chief representative and Mendi Msimang as his deputy. Tambo was based in Tanzania for about three years from 1964 to 1967, half the time in Dar es Salaam and half in Morogoro.

Tanzania, MK and Kongwa

Whether he was in Dar es Salaam or Morogoro, Tambo was never very close to the MK camp at Kongwa, which was about 400 kilometres from the former and 200 kilometres from the latter, and he was only an occasional visitor. Problems with the management of MK began to emerge at Kongwa in 1964–5, and they were to recur later in Zambia and, more dramatically, in Angola in the 1980s. These stemmed from the way in which MK had been set up as a quasi-autonomous organisation and the continuing ambiguity about the relationship between the political and military leaderships. It is unlikely that Tambo either saw himself or was recognised by others at this time as 'commander-in-chief' of MK. This grand title was conferred on the Tswana-speaking Joe Modise, the army commander in Tanzania in 1965, as a way of bolstering his position in relation to the isiXhosa-speaking Kongwa camp commander, Ambrose Makiwane (known as Mbobo, or sjambok, from his propensity for flogging). His appointment was also an answer to those who felt that MK was dominated by isiXhosa-speaking commanders – Moses Mabhida, an isiZulu-speaker, became chief of staff.

Makiwane was a difficult subordinate who refused to take orders from anyone, and was eventually removed and replaced by two other Xhosa-speakers in succession – Joseph Jack and Archie Sibeko (also known as Zola

Zembe). Ethnic tensions at Kongwa were a by-product of the isolation of the camps, the brutal discipline initiated by Makiwane, and the frustration of the men, and a few women, who had been trained militarily in the Soviet Union and elsewhere, but were unable to get into action in South Africa. Tambo's comments on the monthly report from Kongwa camp for December 1965 illustrate some of these problems, and also demonstrate the tentative way in which he felt constrained to deal with the issues.

Tambo suggested that it would be better not to identify 'comrades' by province and urged that every effort should be made to break up ethnic cliques and to counter any tendency towards provincialism. An effort should also be made to introduce literacy classes and political education lectures. He insisted that future reports should include reports on trials leading to corporal punishment 'and more severe penalties' – it is not clear what these were, nor is it clear where the commanders of MK got the idea that flogging was a suitable punishment for soldiers. It is open to question whether this reflected current practice in South African schools or whether it was copied from the practice in other liberation movements at Kongwa.

Tambo complained that the report gave the impression that corporal punishment was administered without the offender being brought before a tribunal and that 'the number of strokes seems to be fixed arbitrarily, according to the momentary mood of a commander'. He asked for this practice to be reviewed and also 'whether 10 strokes and more should not be reserved for very serious offences' and 'whether more use should not be made of penalties other than corporal'.

The lack of a proper disciplinary code or system of tribunals was to be a continuing problem in MK. The adoption of a code in 1979, and of a more comprehensive one in 1985, did not solve the problem of discipline. It is clear that Tambo felt unable to do more than make suggestions about the management of the camp. He did not feel able to impose his views on MK, and there was also a question mark over Joe Modise's ability to control the commanders at Kongwa, where there were in 1966–7 both low-key mutinies and desertions.

Wankie and Sipolilo

The ANC expected that the independence of Botswana on 30 September 1966 would clear the way for the return of MK personnel to South Africa. But the new government of the country, led by Seretse Khama, immediately made it clear that it had no intention of jeopardising its relationship with its powerful neighbour by allowing its territory to be used by the ANC for the return of freedom fighters. Attention then turned to settler Rhodesia, which had declared UDI (Unilateral Declaration of Independence) in November 1965. The idea of a joint movement southwards across the Zambezi had first come up in discussions between rank-and-file members of MK and of the Zimbabwe African People's

Union (ZAPU), which also had a camp at Kongwa. Some members of MK, including Joe Modise, moved south in 1966 to Zambia, where Chris Hani had moved in the middle of the previous year.

The planning of what became the Wankie Campaign was carried out by Joe Modise and Chris Hani for MK, and Akim Ndlovu and Dumiso Dabengwa for ZAPU, with the help of others, but the ANC–ZAPU alliance was concluded at the political level by Tambo for the ANC and James Chikerema for ZAPU in April 1967. As Tambo later commented: 'Military alliance is a big word. But it's not as if we sat down and signed a great big document with clauses and terms. We had close political relations with ZAPU, and these developed into relations at the military level, until we were in a position to fight together.' Tambo was closely involved in the planning and moved to Zambia in mid-1967, with the bulk of the MK personnel, in preparation for the launching of the campaign. Lusaka was to remain his primary base for the next twenty-two years.

5

From Wankie and Sipolilo to Soweto, 1967–76

There was debate at the time, and there has been continuing debate, as to the wisdom of sending MK and ZAPU men across the Zambezi in large groups, without adequate reconnaissance or political preparation, in the hope of establishing what Chris Hani later called a 'Ho Chi Minh' trail to South Africa.

The launching of the expedition was delayed for a week by the news of the death in an accident of Chief Albert Luthuli. Tambo, who became acting president of the ANC on Luthuli's death, named the MK contingent the Luthuli Combat Detachment (LCD) in memory of the late 'Chief'. The group of seventy-nine men finally crossed the Zambezi at the Batoka near Livingstone on the night of 31 July/1 August 1967. They were sent on their way by ANC leaders Tambo, Thomas Nkobi and Joe Modise and by ZAPU leaders Akim Ndlovu and Dumiso Dabengwa.

In later comments Tambo made it clear that the Wankie Campaign was launched in response to pressure from below and was not seen by the ANC as an invasion of Rhodesia: 'it must be remembered that the LCD was not an invasion army. It was a guerrilla detachment expected to avoid battle except when this was impracticable. It had orders not to surrender, but no orders to seek out the enemy and engage it in battle.'

The MK–ZAPU force split into two halves and both clashed with Rhodesian forces. There are no precise figures but approximately thirty men were killed in action or died of wounds, thirty men took refuge in Botswana, and about twenty were taken prisoner and eventually put on trial in Rhodesia. The joint action was acknowledged in a statement by Tambo and Chikerema in Lusaka on 19 August 1967. Undeterred by these losses, a second and larger contingent moved across the Zambezi in December–January 1967–8 in what became known as the Sipolilo Campaign. According to Rhodesian sources, fifty-eight members of the combined force, including fifteen MK men, were killed in action and thirty-eight were taken prisoner.

ANC publications such as *Mayibuye*, which was produced in Lusaka, made grossly exaggerated claims for Rhodesian losses in these actions, but there was no public acknowledgement of MK losses or the number of men taken prisoner. When MK veterans of the Wankie

Campaign, who had been imprisoned in Botswana for entering the country while carrying weapons of war, began to return to Lusaka in September 1968, they expressed shock at the lack of recognition accorded to 'the heroes and martyrs' of Wankie and Sipolilo, and the lack of interest shown in the lessons to be learned from the campaigns.

The Hani Memorandum and the Morogoro Conference

This prompted the writing of what became known as the Hani Memorandum in January 1969 and a major crisis in MK and the ANC in exile. The memorandum, which was signed by Chris Hani and six others, did not name Tambo in person, but it was highly critical of the political leadership of the ANC in exile as a whole, and of Duma Nokwe, the secretary-general, in particular. It maintained that the political leadership, in other words Tambo and the NEC, had lost control of MK, and had allowed Joe Modise, the commander-in-chief, to run it in an arbitrary way. Members of MK had 'lost all confidence in the leadership of the A.N.C.'. The memorandum also referred to 'the emergence of extremely reactionary methods of punishment in M.K.'. It was critical of the salaries that were being paid to senior political and military leaders and alleged that the leadership of the ANC in exile had become a group of globe-trotting professional politicians, which had lost sight of the home front. Tambo saw the reference to the 'fossilization' of the external leadership as an unjustified reflection on Moses Kotane, who had recently suffered a stroke, and on J.B. Marks. The reference to people holding positions to which they had been elected at conferences inside South Africa a decade previously could be seen as referring to both Nokwe and Tambo himself.

At a general meeting of the ANC membership at a ZAPU camp near Lusaka in February 1969, Tambo accepted responsibility for the failings of the leadership and announced the calling of a national consultative conference at Morogoro in April – a response to the final demand of the memorandum. Meanwhile, the signatories were themselves summoned to appear before a tribunal individually and, when they refused to do so, were expelled from the organisation. They were unable, therefore, to attend the Morogoro Conference, but were reinstated soon afterwards. Tambo's initial response to the memorandum was tough, but Chris Hani noted that he had in the end softened his response, stepping back from vindictive action against internal criticism.

In his opening speech at the Morogoro Conference, Tambo acknowledged that one of the main issues confronting the organisation was 'the loss of confidence in the men who have been leading our struggle from Lusaka'. After some criticism from the floor, he dramatically resigned and left the meeting. Following a unanimous vote of confidence in his leadership, he was persuaded to return to the meeting on the following day and was chosen, with J.B. Marks and Moses Mabhida, as a three-man 'president-in-council' to choose a new nine-member NEC.

The main loser in a radical reshuffle was Duma Nokwe, who lost his place on the NEC and his position as secretary-general, to Alfred Nzo. Joe Modise lost the title of commander-in-chief to Tambo, but remained as MK commander. His supporters resented what they saw as his demotion, and in August 1969 Tambo had to deal with a second memorandum from Sotho-Tswana-speaking members of MK in Lusaka who objected to the reinstatement of Hani and his fellow signatories. Tambo demonstrated then, as he did on other occasions, his ability to take personal criticism – he took careful notes of allegations of tribalism and other failings directed against himself.

In an attempt to reduce the pressure in Lusaka, about seventy MK members were then sent to the USSR for further training. In the following year, 1970, thirty MK members were expelled when they refused an order, passed on from the Zambian government, that they should withdraw from Lusaka to a bush camp in preparation for the Non-Aligned Conference. Among those expelled at this time were at least one signatory of the Hani Memorandum and several veterans of Wankie and Sipolilo. Tambo, who was under strong pressure from the Zambian government, took a firm line, saying that by refusing to obey orders these men had effectively expelled themselves.

The most important decision made by the Morogoro Conference was to open membership of the ANC in exile to people of all races. This implied the dissolution of the Congress Alliance, which had already ceased to function. Some members of the Coloured People's Congress, including Barney Desai and Lionel Morrison, had joined the PAC in Tanzania after they were refused individual membership of the ANC. The NEC remained closed to non-Africans, but a new Revolutionary Council, which was non-racial, was established. The conference adopted a 'Strategy and tactics' document, which rejected 'all manifestations of militarism' and, in a concession to one of the major themes of the Hani Memorandum, acknowledged that 'the primacy of the political leadership is unchallenged and supreme'. Chris Hani later hailed the 'Strategy and tactics' document as 'the lodestar of our movement', but Mac Maharaj remained sceptical. In his view it was another decade before the primacy of the political was really established after the visit of Tambo, Slovo, Modise and others to Vietnam in 1978.

The Morogoro Conference strengthened Tambo's position as leader of the ANC, but he immediately faced another crisis in the shape of the Lusaka Manifesto. Through this declaration, which was issued in April 1969, the East and Central African states, including the ANC's two most important host countries, Zambia and Tanzania, stepped back from support for confrontation with South Africa. From that date onwards, neither country allowed MK to have training camps on its territory. A further complication was the enforced removal of the remnants of MK from Kongwa to the USSR in September 1969.

This was a consequence of the PAC leader Potlako Leballo's successful attempt to implicate Tambo in a coup plot, which was allegedly masterminded by Oscar Kambona, the former chairman of the OAU's Liberation Committee. Leballo suggested that Tambo had knowledge of the plot, which he had not passed on to the Tanzanian authorities. Tambo declined to give evidence in the case, but said later that he could only have done so for the defence. It was almost two years before relations between Nyerere, who leaned towards the PAC, and Tambo were restored and some MK members were allowed to return to Kongwa. They were not, however, permitted to be militarily active. It was only some time after the independence of Angola in 1975 that MK was able to set up military camps, and it remained militarily inactive in South Africa until 1977.

Challenge to Tambo's leadership

The most outspoken critic of the decision to open the ANC in exile to people of all races was Tennyson Makiwane, who emerged over the next few years as the leader of an opposition faction, which also included Ambrose Makiwane and Alfred Kgokong. At a special

'Africans only' meeting in Lusaka in August 1971 – seen by Joe Slovo as intended to exclude members of the SACP, such as himself – Tambo sought to pin the blame for the problems that the ANC had experienced since Morogoro in Tanzania, Zambia and London on the machinations of Ambrose Makiwane and Kgokong, who had both been suspended from the NEC before the Morogoro Conference.

London was the main centre of opposition to the opening of the ANC, and there was criticism of the appointment of Reg September as the chief representative there in succession to Mazisi Kunene, on the grounds that he could not, as a coloured person, project an 'African image'. Open conflict broke out in July 1975 at the service for the unveiling of the tombstone for Robert Resha, who had died there in 1973. Tambo had attended his funeral service in that year, which was conducted by Canon Collins in St Paul's Cathedral.

Alfred Kgokong and Ambrose Makiwane both spoke at the unveiling and claimed that Resha had been the victim of a 'non-African' and communist clique that had hijacked the ANC in exile. Makiwane demanded that the ANC should be redirected to 'its true nationalist course'. Among those present at the ceremony was Duma Nokwe, who had worked his way back to the position of deputy secretary-general after his demotion at Morogoro in 1969. He was infuriated by what he saw as the hijacking of Resha's memory – and by the challenge to Tambo's leadership. At a meeting of the NEC in Lusaka in September 1975 it was decided to expel the two Makiwanes, Kgokong and five others including Jonas Matlou. They came to be known collectively as the Gang of Eight.

In his published letter of protest at the expulsions, Tennyson Makiwane complained bitterly that they had not been given the chance to defend themselves – there had been no due process. According to Luli Callinicos, Tambo himself voted against the expulsions, but accepted the majority view in the NEC. Joe Slovo and Jack Simons also questioned the procedure. Nelson Mandela regretted the expulsions, but, in a letter that was smuggled from Robben Island in the following year, he stated: 'There is only one ANC and that is the ANC which has its head office in Lusaka, and whose president is O[liver] T[ambo].' Mac Maharaj, who was then also on Robben Island, thought that the expulsions were a mistake, but he believed that Tambo learned from them and resolved to take a firmer line with the NEC in future.

The expelled group sought to establish a rival organisation, the ANC (African Nationalists), which was launched in London in December 1975. They had very little support and the group soon disintegrated – most of its members were readmitted to the ANC in the mid-1980s. The group's statements included strong criticisms of Tambo's leadership. They accused him of failing to react promptly to events in Portugal, Angola and Mozambique, or to the South African government's détente initiative, which had been launched in response to those events in 1974. They accused him of failing to deal with big issues like the 'interference' of the SACP in the affairs of the ANC. His lack of militarism and his consensual style were, unfairly, held against him. They contrasted Tambo, 'his hand clutching a passport, always on the point of flying off somewhere', unfavourably with the Mozambican leader, Samora Machel, 'who during the struggle was seen always having a gun slung over his shoulder leading his men into the fight'. They further asserted: 'It is our considered view that Oliver Tambo has clearly betrayed the sacred trust and mandate given him by the ANC to head the external mission ... No, the truth must be said as it is ... Oliver Tambo is unfit to lead a revolutionary struggle.'

At least half of the expelled members were former members of the SACP, which came out strongly against them in a lengthy statement entitled 'The enemy hidden under the same colour'. Tambo did not think that the question of open membership was the real issue. He later commented: 'They just wanted to be leaders – that is all. It was a power struggle.'

From détente to Soweto

It was not a coincidence that this somewhat forlorn challenge to Tambo's leadership came at one of the lowest points in the history of the ANC in exile – the moment of détente between the revolution in Portugal in April 1974 and the Soweto Uprising in June 1976. It is a tribute to Tambo's extraordinary resilience that in the early 1970s he not only had to overcome ethnic and other problems within MK and a challenge to his leadership, but had also to contend with the continuing indifference of the ANC's two most important host countries, Zambia and Tanzania.

It was symptomatic of the lack of priority given to the ANC in Zambia that it was unable to persuade President Kaunda, Grey Zulu, the minister of defence, or Aaron Milner, secretary-general to the government and Kaunda's main link with the half-dozen liberation movements then based in Zambia, to attend the celebration of its sixtieth anniversary in Lusaka in 1972. It had to make do with a deputy minister for rural affairs, who had once been a member of the ANC Youth League in Johannesburg, as the government's representative.

In February 1974, the organisation's deputy chief representative in Zambia, John Dube (MK name of Adolphus Boy Mvemve), was killed by a parcel bomb, which destroyed the ANC office at the Liberation Centre. The coup in Portugal in April, which heralded the independence of Angola and Mozambique, offered a chink of light, but it was immediately followed by South Africa's attempt at détente through which Prime Minister B.J. Vorster sought to 'solve' the issues of Rhodesia and South West Africa.

The Front Line States of Zambia, Tanzania and

Botswana, together with Samora Machel, the president of FRELIMO (Mozambique Liberation Front) and the future president of Mozambique, were all involved, directly or indirectly, in this process. At his second meeting with Vorster in October 1974, Kaunda's chief envoy, Mark Chona, gave an assurance that he had it on the authority of the four presidents that none of them would allow Oliver Tambo a 'programme for training' or a base from which to attack South Africa.

On 16 December 1974, the MK anniversary, Tambo told a commemorative meeting that the ANC's sidelining in the talks that were then taking place at State House in Lusaka between representatives of the Front Line States, including Nyerere, and Rhodesian representatives amounted to 'a calculated rejection'. At the time of the meeting between Vorster and Kaunda at the Victoria Falls in August 1975, when the discussion related mainly to Rhodesia and Angola, Tambo told representatives of the Swedish government that Kaunda had 'gone out of his way to accommodate Vorster'. The ANC in Zambia had been reduced to an information and propaganda role, but even that had been restricted by the temporary closing down of Radio Freedom, which had begun broadcasting on short wave from Lusaka in 1973. He concluded: 'they may ask us to leave, but until then we intend to stay.'

South Africa's invasion of Angola, Cuban intervention, and South Africa's enforced withdrawal in January 1976 put an end to détente and had an impact, as did Mozambique's independence in September 1975, on public opinion inside South Africa. There was a clear link between these events and the Soweto Uprising, which erupted on 16 June 1976 after a build-up of tension in schools over Bantu Education and the use of Afrikaans as a medium of instruction. The ANC in exile had always found it difficult to keep up with events and political change inside South Africa, but Tambo had made some moves in 1973–5 that ensured that the ANC was relatively well placed to take advantage of the exodus of about four thousand young refugees that took place in 1976–7.

In what turned out to be a stroke of genius, he had sent two of the brightest and youngest members of the NEC to the former protectorates, Botswana, Lesotho and Swaziland, to begin the work of rebuilding the underground inside South Africa. Tambo had met Seretse Khama in 1973, probably through Joe Matthews, who had moved to Botswana in 1970, and almost immediately afterwards sent Thabo Mbeki, a young British-trained economics graduate and the son of Robben Island prisoner Govan Mbeki, to Botswana, where he spent most of a year. During that time he was able to make contact with leading members of the Black Consciousness Movement. There were plans for Tambo to meet Steve Biko in Botswana in 1976, but these were postponed. Biko's murder in police detention in 1977 is widely believed to have been related to renewed plans for a high-level meeting with the ANC.

Tambo also had direct contacts with Bantustan leaders in London and elsewhere. In 1973, for example, he met with Gatsha Buthelezi, Kaiser Matanzima and Lucas Mangope in London, and with Buthelezi again in Nairobi. He later acknowledged that he had encouraged Buthelezi to re-establish the Inkatha cultural movement in 1975 – an organisation that Buthelezi presented for a while as the 'internal wing' of the ANC. The relationship between Buthelezi and the ANC was always tense, as he opposed both armed struggle and sanctions, and it broke down irretrievably when he publicised what was supposed to be a confidential meeting between the KwaZulu 'cabinet' and leaders of the ANC, including Tambo, in London in October 1979.

In January 1975 Mbeki was able to travel through Mozambique, which was not yet independent, to Swaziland, which provided good access to Johannesburg, Natal and the Eastern Cape. Over the next eighteen months, until his deportation in June 1976, he worked with Stanley Mabizela to reopen lines of communication and make contact with ANC underground cells. Tambo himself was able to travel to Swaziland in July 1975 and established a good relationship with King Sobhuza II, who saw himself as a lifelong member of the ANC because of the involvement of his grandmother, Queen Labotsibeni, and his uncle, Prince Malunge, in its foundation in 1912. In spite of Tambo's good relationship with Sobhuza, the position of the ANC in Swaziland was never easy. The country was, however, to be vital for the transit of people from South Africa through Mozambique to Zambia and the north – and in the reverse direction. Mbeki's establishment of an ANC presence and profile in Swaziland was to prove important in the aftermath of the Soweto Uprising.

At about the same time that Tambo and the NEC had sent Mbeki to Botswana and Swaziland, they sent Chris Hani, another rising star, through South Africa to Lesotho, which he reached in December 1974. He had some difficulty in establishing himself in the country, but he was able to stay for over seven years and played a major role in the rebuilding of the ANC in the Free State and in the Eastern and Western Cape. He also played an important part in the building of trade unions and civic associations, which were, from 1983 onwards, to form some of the building blocks for the United Democratic Front (UDF).

As a result of these moves, Tambo and the ANC in Lusaka were by 1976 much better informed about developments inside South Africa, whether in the Bantustans, emergent trade unions or the Black Consciousness Movement and student organisations, than they might otherwise have been. It is usually estimated that about two-thirds of the students who left South Africa in 1976–7 joined the ANC and were sent on by it to Angola for military training, or to Tanzania for further education. Zanele Mbeki, who was then working for the Scandinavian-backed International

University Exchange Fund (IUEF), recalls how hard Tambo worked to find funds and educational places in Nigeria and elsewhere for members of the Soweto generation. He was never sectarian in his approach to finding educational opportunities for South African exiles and saw little difference between the political position of the Black Consciousness Movement and that of the ANC Youth League in the 1940s.

It was of vital importance for the reception of the Soweto students that Tambo had been able to convince the Scandinavian countries to provide the ANC with direct support. He had met Olof Palme in Lusaka in 1971 and had travelled to Sweden in 1972. There had, as we have seen, been earlier contacts, but Tambo had to overcome prejudices on the part of the Swedish Social Democratic Party and the trade unions, which had been doubtful about the ANC–SACP alliance and about SACTU's membership of the Soviet-aligned World Federation of Trade Unions, before funds began to flow. Humanitarian aid from the Swedish International Development Agency (SIDA) to the ANC began on a small scale in 1972 and built up very rapidly from 1976 onwards. From then until the end of exile, Swedish aid accounted for almost half of the ANC's cash income. Without large-scale Scandinavian support, the ANC would not have been able to fund the reception of the members of the Soweto generation or to establish the Solomon Mahlangu Freedom College (Somafco) at Mazimbu, near Morogoro in Tanzania.

6

From Angola to Kabwe, 1977–85

As a result of direct negotiations between Tambo and President Agostinho Neto, the ANC was allowed to set up military training camps in Angola, which were initially under Cuban control. Angola was far from an ideal base because it was the scene of an on-going civil war between the MPLA (People's Movement for the Liberation of Angola) and UNITA (National Union for the Total Independence of Angola), and there were also problems within the MPLA. The arrival of the first contingent of trainees at Novo Catengue, near Benguela, in April 1977 coincided almost exactly with the suppression in Luanda of a coup attempt by, and demonstrations in support of, the MPLA leader Nito Alves. Zambia, Tanzania and Mozambique would have been more suitable places for ANC camps, but none of these countries was prepared to accommodate MK.

Tambo was the nominal commander-in-chief of MK, but he paid only occasional visits to the camps. As MK commander, Joe Modise spent some time in Angola in 1977–8, but he was usually based in Lusaka. Joe Slovo, MK's chief of staff, was based from 1977 to 1984 in Maputo, while spending some time in Lusaka. Chris Hani was in Lesotho until 1982 and then divided his time until 1984 between Lusaka, Angola and Mozambique. Tambo delegated overall responsibility for MK in Angola to Mzwai Piliso, who was in charge of personnel and training from 1977 to 1981, and Andrew Masondo, former Robben Island prisoner and Fort Hare maths lecturer, who was national commissar from 1977 to 1985.

The camp commanders were usually both young and inexperienced – as were the people charged with responsibility for security. The absence of the senior commanders, poor living conditions, the lack of medical facilities, brutal discipline, and the increasingly adversarial role of the security department, all contributed to tension. The fundamental problem was, however, the deep frustration of the men, and a few women, who were desperate to put their military training to use in action in South Africa, but were unable to do so because of the lack of a supportive political underground.

A new emphasis on political preparation inside South Africa arose as a result of the visit of Tambo, Modise, Slovo and others to Vietnam in October 1978, during which they had a meeting with the renowned strategist

General Giáp. Tambo told a combined meeting of the NEC and the Revolutionary Council in Luanda in December–January 1978–9 that MK's efforts had come to nothing because of the lack of political work. Slovo wanted a clear statement of the precedence of the political over the military, but Tambo sidestepped this suggestion and called for a Morogoro-style national consultative conference. A committee was set up to work on the guidelines for that, but, for reasons that remain obscure, the conference did not happen until 1985.

A Politico-Military Strategy Commission was set up in January 1979, which produced a report known as the 'Green Book'. The report, which included a blueprint for the establishment of a mass-based movement along the lines of the later United Democratic Front, was debated at a meeting in Maputo later in 1979. Among the other issues discussed was a suggestion from Joe Slovo that the ANC should turn itself into a Marxist-Leninist party like FRELIMO or the MPLA. Perhaps surprisingly, Tambo, who had been impressed by the freedom permitted to the churches in Vietnam, was prepared to go along with this suggestion. Thabo Mbeki pointed out that this would require the dissolution of the SACP, and Moses Mabhida, who was about to be confirmed as its general secretary, rejected the suggestion. In the wake of this report there was a new emphasis on armed propaganda, and the special operations unit, under the overall command of Joe Slovo, achieved some of MK's most spectacular successes, including the attack on Sasol II in 1980.

The huge expansion in the number of people for whom the ANC in exile had responsibility in 1976–7 – from hundreds to thousands – revealed serious weaknesses in its bureaucratic structures. There were large new projects such as Somafco in Tanzania and Chongela Farm near Lusaka, and the organisation had to deal with hard-headed donors like the Swedes. Tambo, with the help of Thabo Mbeki, who became his political secretary in January 1978 and remained his right-hand man until 1989, produced a scathing presidential report on these weaknesses in May 1979.

This report, which was discussed at a meeting of the NEC in Dar es Salaam in August, emphasised the urgent need to strengthen the offices of the president-general, the secretary-general and the treasurer-general, which were all described as 'dismally weak'. It also pointed to the serious weaknesses in the Internal Political and Reconstruction Department, and in the Department of Information and Publicity, which was described as in the process of formation. Mbeki was himself the head of this department, though his duties in the president's office took up much of his time. The Education and Health departments were in the process of formation, and the Security Department was described as 'a fledgling and largely amateur outfit'.

There were also continuing problems with the political control of MK. The Morogoro Conference had set up a Revolutionary Council, which was supposed to manage MK, but it rarely met, and its subcommittees had taken on lives of their own. It was only in 1983 that a new Political-Military Council was set up and a military headquarters was established in Lusaka.

Trouble in Angola

There can be no doubt that things went badly wrong for the ANC in Angola in 1980–4, in relation to both security and the management of the camps. There can equally be no doubt that Tambo was fully aware of the weaknesses of ANC security in 1979–80. He complained bitterly to the secretary-general, Alfred Nzo, who had overall responsibility for security, which was then being run by Simon Makana, about a variety of issues including the refusal of the London office to give the historian Martin Legassick security clearance for work in Mozambique, and of the NWC to clear Ben Turok for work in Lusaka. He also complained in 1980 about the brutal treatment by security of ANC students in Tanzania who had returned from the Soviet Union.

It is not entirely clear why Tambo felt unable to intervene directly in these cases or to stop the investigation by security in 1979–80 of Thabo Mbeki's involvement in the making of a prize-winning film, *The Battle for South Africa*, by CBS News – a film which had been set up by Johnny Makatini in the United States and in which Tambo had himself participated. Nzo eventually put out a circular clearing Mbeki of suspicion, but it offered no criticism of the Security Department, which was prone to both anti-American and anti-British paranoia. The revelation that Craig Williamson, who had worked closely with the ANC while acting as deputy director of the IUEF, was a South African agent, was also a source of embarrassment – especially since the ANC had failed to pass on its suspicions about him to the Swedish government.

A major crisis over security came in 1980–1 with the exposure, as a result of the Zambian investigation of a coup attempt, of what appeared to be a South African spy ring operating within the ANC in Lusaka. Tambo's own response to this revelation was one of incredulity. This discovery coincided with the South African Defence Force raid on Matola in Mozambique in January 1981 and the disarmament of the ANC in Lusaka. Several hundred 'suspects' were rounded up in Zambia and the region and then transferred to Angola. At least four people died during interrogation in Angola and there were several executions there of suspected spies. The Security Department, now led by Piliso, produced an unconvincing report, known as the Shishita report, in July 1981. While detailing various alleged plots and conspiracies, it equated criticism of the leadership with subversion.

There was a direct link between this crisis and the two mutinies that occurred in 1984 in Angola. The problems that had been identified there in 1981 had been allowed to fester, and Angola had become a dumping ground for 'suspects'. The situation there was made worse by MK's involvement in the war with UNITA and then, in March 1984, by the Nkomati Accord between South Africa and Mozambique, which threatened to close down the access route to South Africa by way of Mozambique and Swaziland.

Following the first of these mutinies, Tambo acted with exceptional speed to appoint a commission of inquiry under the leadership of James Stuart (MK name of Hermanus Loots), and included Aziz Pahad and Sizakele Sigxashe. It carried out interviews on the spot and produced a devastatingly critical report within weeks. This spoke of 'a nearly total collapse of the political, military and moral organisation in Angola' with resultant 'confusion, fear and lawlessness', and concluded that there were sufficient genuine grievances to explain the mutiny without recourse to conspiracy theories involving 'enemy agents'. The report further concluded that what was needed was not punitive action, but political work, without which there would, it accurately predicted, be another mutiny.

The report recommended that there should be a 'national consultative conference', as Tambo had first proposed in 1979 and as the mutineers had demanded, and that the members of the 'Committee of Ten', the elected representatives of the mutineers, should be released from Luanda maximum security prison. The conference was called and took place in June 1985, but the members of the committee were not immediately released. Some were released after a year, but the majority were then transferred to what became known as Quatro – an ANC prison camp near Quibaxe, which took its name from Johannesburg's Fort or 'Number 4' prison, and acquired similar notoriety.

Tambo's detailed examination of the Stuart Report survives and demonstrates his superior powers of forensic analysis. He was clearly shocked and, at times, incredulous about what he read. He was impressed by the commission's conclusion that the mutiny was not organised by enemy agents and he noted that the members of the Committee of Ten had been elected by their comrades. He was clearly disturbed to read that Masondo and Piliso had threatened members of MK, who had responded critically to his request for feedback in 1982, with disciplinary action. In the course of the discussion of the report by the NWC, Joe Modise acknowledged that too much power and responsibility had been placed in the hands of young and inexperienced people in the Security Department. Their methods had been too harsh and had resulted in deaths: 'We knew this and we did not intervene.'

Although the ANC had subscribed to the Geneva Convention in 1980 at a solemn ceremony at the headquarters of the International Red Cross, in which Tambo participated, there was still no proper judicial process. The thirty or so people who were executed as enemy agents or mutineers, or who were convicted (however insecurely) of rape or murder, between 1981 and 1984, had no legal defence or right of appeal. There was a euphemistic reference to the 'maximum penalty' in the code of conduct that was adopted in 1979, and it may have been thought that no special permission to carry out executions was needed. Only at the Kabwe Conference in June 1985 were rules drawn up requiring the authorisation of executions by the NWC – only three executions were carried out after that date, not all of them according to the prescribed procedure.

Tambo was clearly aware that executions were being carried out, though he may not have been informed in all cases until after the event. According to James Stuart, who presided over a commission investigating the release of detainees from Quatro in 1985–6, Tambo was personally opposed to the death penalty and stopped at least one execution at that time. He had also intervened through Gertrude Shope, and on the insistence of Chris Hani, to stop the executions that were being carried out after the second of the mutinies in 1984. Albie Sachs was shocked to hear Tambo's frank acknowledgement around the time of the Kabwe Conference that the ANC was using torture. Clearly, things were happening in Angola at this time, sometimes as the result of Angolan government pressure, over which neither Tambo nor the NEC had total control. As will emerge later, some people, including Chris Hani, thought that Tambo acted too slowly to stop the abuses in Angola.

The personal price

There was undoubtedly a relationship between the crises in Angola and the breakdown in Tambo's health. According to E.S. Reddy, writing from New York to Trevor Huddleston in October 1984, Tambo had a series of three heart attacks in November–December 1983, as the crisis in Angola was beginning, and then had a period of rest in the English countryside. He had a stroke in Dar es Salaam in September 1984 and spent some time in hospital there and in Lusaka before spending a month in a sanatorium in the Soviet Union. Between the heart attacks and the stroke he had to contend with the second, and the more serious, of the Angolan mutinies, and also with one of the greatest diplomatic setbacks that the ANC in exile faced at any time – the Nkomati Accord of March 1984 – and its repercussions. This can be compared for the shock of its impact with the Lusaka Manifesto in 1969. In his concluding speech at the Kabwe Conference in June 1985, Tambo said: 'Comrades, my health has not been best of late, but what is left of it will be consumed for the struggle.'

7

Towards negotiations: From Kabwe to Harare, 1985–93

In an interview with Luli Callinicos in 2002, Thabo Mbeki recalled Oliver Tambo's recurring nightmare – that the apartheid regime would send a signal saying, 'We want to talk. We want to sit down with you and make an agreement to end the system of apartheid', and that the ANC would fail to understand the message. 'We would end up in a situation of greater disaster, whereas the situation could have been rescued.'

These signals began to arrive in the last four or five years of Tambo's active life. In spite of failing health, he was then able to demonstrate his extraordinary skills both in relation to the management of the ANC and as an international statesman. Only then did he begin to receive the belated and grudging recognition of the Western powers – something that he had been denied since the early

1960s – and have contact for the first time at the highest level with the leaders of the Soviet Union and China.

There can be no doubt that the Nkomati Accord – a non-aggression pact between Mozambique and South Africa – was a major setback for the ANC. But it was also a turning point, attracting sympathy for the organisation from other members of the Front Line States, especially Zambia and Tanzania. Both Nyerere and Kaunda were impressed by the magnanimity with which Tambo accepted the accord and expressed their appreciation of this at a special meeting in Arusha in April 1984. Tambo was personally closer to Kaunda after Nkomati than ever before. By the beginning of 1986 he had moved into State House in Lusaka – he and Adelaide had spent the previous Christmas with the Kaunda family at Kasaba Bay on Lake Tanganyika.

There was almost certainly a link between the accord and the stay-aways and strikes, which began in the Vaal Triangle in September 1984, subsequently spread throughout South Africa, and culminated in the regime's declaration of a partial state of emergency in July 1985. When Tambo, speaking on Radio Freedom on 8 January 1985, the ANC's anniversary, called upon the people of South Africa to make the country 'ungovernable', he was responding to the situation that was evolving on the ground. But he was also speaking to a larger and more receptive audience in South Africa, organised through the UDF, than ever before.

Five months later, on 16 June 1985, the ninth anniversary of the Soweto Uprising, Tambo opened the national consultative conference at Kabwe in central Zambia. Preparations for this had been going on for most of a year and involved a series of regional conferences at which issues of concern were discussed and delegates to the main conference were elected. Tambo was determined that this should be a truly democratic process, but there was some anxiety that the conference, which was attended by about 250 delegates from all over the world, might prove to be divisive.

The commanders of the camps in Angola had made a determined effort to pack the regional conference and the MK delegation to the Kabwe Conference itself with 'loyalists', but they were not entirely successful. As a result of the intervention of Chris Hani and Ronnie Kasrils, some critical voices from Angola, including that of Stanley Manong, were heard. Sensing the mood of the meeting, which was critical, Tambo supplemented Nzo's bland secretary-general's report on the Security Department with something more hard-hitting. He noted that: 'Some of the comrades manning these organs have made bad, sometimes terrible mistakes. They have over-reacted in some situations and have employed unacceptable methods, thus distorting the image of the Department of Intelligence and Security.' The demand from some of the camp delegates that the Stuart Report should be made available to all was, however, opposed by Chris Hani, who clearly thought that its circulation would be damaging to the leadership of MK.

The most important decision made at the conference was to open membership of the NEC to members of all races. The holders of the top three jobs, Tambo, Nzo and Nkobi, were re-elected by acclamation. Among those elected to the new NEC were Joe Slovo, Reg September, James Stuart, Mac Maharaj and Aziz Pahad. Andrew Masondo was not re-elected to the NEC and, receiving most of the blame for what had gone wrong in Angola, also lost his job as national commissar. All the twenty-seven elected members of the NEC were chosen from a list of forty that Tambo provided at the request of the delegates, but many candidates who were not on his list also stood.

The conference adopted a new constitution and a more elaborate code of conduct, which provided for a system of tribunals and appeals. Torture was outlawed, but, controversially, 'intensive measures of interrogation' were permitted in certain circumstances. The 'maximum penalty', a euphemism for the death penalty, remained in the code. An 'officer of justice', Zola Skweyiya, was appointed to supervise the new system, but he was to have great difficulty in asserting his authority over the Security Department. It was not until 1987 that Mzwai Piliso was replaced as head of security and that Tambo himself visited Quatro.

For Joel Netshitenzhe and Thabo Mbeki, the most important decision of the conference related to the intensification of 'people's war' in the context of the rise of the UDF and the upsurge of popular protest in South Africa. At a press conference Tambo stated with regret that the distinction between 'soft' and 'hard' targets would disappear in 'an intensified confrontation ... an escalating conflict' – but there was no change in the ANC's policy on the avoidance of civilian casualties.

The conference concluded that there could be no question of a negotiated settlement so long as Mandela and other leaders were in prison, but negotiations could not be ruled out entirely. A subcommittee was appointed to look into the question. According to Howard Barrell, who was at the conference, Tambo asked the conference for permission to enter into talks with an unnamed group of 'important people' from South Africa. This was a reference to the 'Anglo American' group of businessmen and journalists which had made its first approach to Tambo through President Kaunda in April 1985.

The Anglo American talks

The arrival of the members of this group, led by Gavin Relly, in Zambia in September proved to be a major turning point for the ANC. They had a day of talks with ANC leaders, including Tambo, Mbeki, Mac Maharaj and Chris Hani, at President Kaunda's lodge at Mfuwe in the Luangwa National Park. The visit has often been seen as a response to President P.W. Botha's failure to 'cross the Rubicon' in an over-hyped speech in August, but it had been planned for some time before that. Tambo made it clear in his opening speech that the ANC took its stand on the Freedom Charter and he stated that 'South Africa belongs to all South Africans and all South Africans belong to South Africa'. He also emphasised that the ANC stood for 'one man one vote in a unitary state', and it would be the object of any negotiations to achieve that.

Tambo was at great pains, as he often was when speaking to a white or Western audience, to explain the ANC's reluctant turn to violence, and its relationship with the SACP, which, he insisted, made no claims to lead the liberation movement. The question was, he said, not whether South Africa would be capitalist or socialist, but would be one of narrowing the gap between the haves and the have-nots through the redistribution of wealth. Tambo correctly predicted that it might take four years before negotiations could begin, but he said the ANC was not opposed to a transitional government of national unity. In the following month he was invited, with Thabo Mbeki and Aziz Pahad, to appear before the Foreign Affairs Committee of the British Parliament. He had, once again, to defend the turn to armed struggle and to justify the call for sanctions. In doing so, he patiently explained the systemic violence of apartheid, and the relative moderation of MK's response.

From this time onwards, things began to move very fast. Within six months, delegations had reached Lusaka from the Progressive Federal Party, led by Frederik van Zyl Slabbert and Alex Boraine, who subsequently resigned from Parliament and set up IDASA (the Institute for a Democratic Alternative for South Africa), the South African Council of Churches, the Soweto Parents Crisis Committee, the South African Catholic Bishops Conference, led by Archbishop Hurley, the Congress of South African Trade Unions (COSATU), led by Jay Naidoo and Chris Dlamini, with Cyril Ramaphosa, and the KaNgwane Bantustan, led by Chief Enos Mabuza. In January 1986 Tambo was present in Stockholm for the first official meeting between the ANC and representatives of the UDF, and it was then that he had his last meeting with Olof Palme. Following Palme's assassination on 28 February, Tambo returned to Sweden in March to speak at his funeral.

He had heard the news of Palme's assassination during a visit to Lusaka by George Bizos, Nelson Mandela's lawyer who had come with the knowledge of Kobie Coetsee, the minister of justice, to brief Tambo on Mandela's decision to enter into talks with the government. On the same day as Bizos's visit to State House, where Tambo had taken up residence for the sake of security, Kaunda had a meeting with General Olusegun Obasanjo, former president of Nigeria, and Malcolm Fraser, prime minister of Australia, who had come as the advance guard of the Commonwealth Eminent Persons Group (EPG). They reported on preliminary meetings they had had with the South African government. Obasanjo had also met Mandela at Pollsmoor prison.

The Eminent Persons Group

The EPG had been set up as part of a compromise, the Nassau Accord, to prevent a damaging split in the Commonwealth, resulting from Margaret Thatcher's total opposition to the imposition of comprehensive sanctions on South Africa. It had taken pressure from Thatcher on P.W. Botha and from Kaunda on Tambo to get the two sides to agree to indirect talks through the mediation of the EPG. By May 1986, the South African government had not responded to the EPG's 'possible negotiating concept', which included the withdrawal of troops from the townships, the release of Mandela and other political prisoners, and the unbanning of the ANC as a preliminary to negotiations and an end to violence.

Mandela indicated that he could personally accept the concept, but would have to consult with leaders of the Mass Democratic Movement (MDM) and with the ANC in Lusaka. Tambo told the EPG that the ANC would need ten days for its own consultations. He said that he had no objection in principle to negotiations, but pointed to South Africa's prevarication over Namibia, and its breaches of the Nkomati and Lusaka accords with Mozambique and Angola. There was some relief in ANC circles when the South African government – specifically General Magnus Malan, the minister of defence, acting on the authority of President Botha, but without reference to the cabinet – wrecked the EPG process by attacks on ANC targets in Botswana, Zimbabwe and Zambia. These attacks were carried out on 19 May while the EPG team was still in South Africa.

In its published report, which came out in June, the EPG expressed the view that the apartheid regime was not yet ready for negotiations and that if it found itself unable to 'talk with men like Mandela and Tambo, the future of South Africa is bleak indeed'. The EPG initiative may have failed, but it led to the recognition of the ANC by the Western powers. Tambo had his first meetings with a senior British Foreign Office official in Lusaka in February 1986 and with a junior minister at the Foreign Office in London, Lynda Chalker, in June. He had met the West German foreign minister, Hans-Dietrich Genscher, in Bonn in April. In September 1986, he had separate meetings on the same day in London with both the British foreign minister, Geoffrey Howe, and the United States assistant secretary of state for Africa, Chester Crocker. The latter meeting paved the way for Tambo's meeting with the secretary of state, George Shultz, in Washington in January 1987 at the end of an American tour.

Lynda Chalker made it clear in a later recollection of her meeting with Tambo that she regarded him as the leader of the ANC's moderates. She was convinced that he 'really was the patient leader, often having to rein in others in the movement'. The meeting with Howe, which also had the approval of Thatcher, took place at his official country residence in Kent. The sight of sheep grazing outside the windows of Chevening House made Tambo feel at home and, according to Howe, he expressed the wish that, on the occasion of a future meeting, he might spend the night there. Sadly, they never met again, but Tambo convinced Howe that the ANC had turned to armed struggle as a last resort. In his recollection of the meeting, Howe described Tambo as 'a man who used real words and gave real answers', and as 'the non-violent supporter of the armed struggle'.

Only after these two meetings with Western European foreign ministers, and after the summit meeting between President Reagan and General Secretary Gorbachev, did Tambo have his first-ever meeting with a Soviet head of government – with Gorbachev in Moscow in November 1986. Although Joe Slovo and Chris Hani accompanied Tambo to Moscow, Thabo Mbeki was the only person who was present with him at the two-hour meeting. By some accounts, Gorbachev told Tambo that there would, as a result of the thaw in relations with the United States, be reduced Soviet support for the ANC and that it should move towards a negotiated settlement. Although the meeting was apparently cordial, a promised follow-up meeting did not take place.

In the last three or four years of his politically active life, Tambo took three important initiatives: setting up a committee to draw up a draft constitution for a liberated, non-racial and democratic South Africa – the constitutional guidelines; setting up an operation to send a member, or members, of the NEC into South Africa – Operation Vula; and drawing up a document for international acceptance on the preconditions for negotiations – the Harare Declaration.

Constitutional guidelines

In January 1986 Tambo appointed his close friend Jack Simons, a long-term Lusaka resident, as chairman of the Constitutional Committee, with Zola Skweyiya as vice-chairman. Its other members included Penuell Maduna, Kader Asmal, then based in Ireland, and Albie Sachs, who was working in Mozambique. Addressing the committee, Tambo stressed that the ANC should have its own proposals on the table to pre-empt those of others, whether the South African government, the United States or the United Kingdom. The constitution should be based on the principles of the Freedom Charter and should make provision for a multiparty electoral system and a 'mixed economy', with an entrenched bill of rights. The committee produced an outline proposal along these lines within a week. It proposed a preamble based on the Freedom Charter and the establishment, as part of the transitional process, of constitutional, affirmative action and public service commissions. It made no specific recommendations on economic issues such as the ownership of the means of production and distribution, the transfer of land, or affirmative action.

The draft was referred to a subcommittee of the NWC, including Joe Slovo and Pallo Jordan, which concluded that it was 'too wedded to liberal-democratic notions' and framed in terms of 'a conventional bourgeois democracy'. The committee responded that the draft was well suited to the first stage of a two-stage revolution – that 'one-man one-vote in a unitary state' was in itself a revolutionary proposal in the context of contemporary South Africa. After a number of meetings and seminars, the revised constitutional guidelines were accepted by the NEC in 1988. As Tambo had intended, they made no reference to revolution, 'people's power' or nationalisation, but they made provision for affirmative action in relation to both race and gender. No less an authority than Fidel Castro had, in the early 1980s, advised Tambo and the ANC against nationalisation on account of the Cuban experience. The guidelines had an influence on the eventual process of negotiations and on both the transitional and final constitutions.

Operation Vula

Mac Maharaj had argued for a long time that it was important to get a member of the NEC into South Africa. The proposal for what became known as Operation Vula was only approved by the NEC in 1987. Tambo was appointed, with Joe Slovo, to supervise it and Maharaj was designated as the leader on the ground. It took a year to set up the operation, which required a great deal of support from the Dutch anti-apartheid movement, targeted funding from donors such as Lord Joffe, and logistical support from the Soviet Union. Maharaj and Siphiwe Nyanda, a long-serving MK commander, finally crossed the Swaziland border into South Africa in August 1988. Operation Vula had a military component and involved the movement of large quantities of arms into South Africa. It proved, however, to be most useful as providing a means of communication between the MDM, Nelson Mandela in Pollsmoor prison, and the ANC in Lusaka. The security of the operation was greatly enhanced because it used computer modems before emails or the internet had been established in South Africa, cutting out the need for couriers. By the middle of 1989, Tambo was in direct communication with Mandela through Maharaj and Vula. Later in the year, Thabo Mbeki, with Tambo's encouragement, made direct contact with Mandela by phone. He was also in contact with his own father, Govan, who had been released from prison in 1987.

The Mells Park talks

At roughly the same time that Operation Vula was being organised, Tambo was closely involved in the setting up of clandestine talks in the UK between members of the Afrikaner intellectual establishment, operating as a channel to the National Intelligence Service (NIS), and leading members of the ANC, including Thabo Mbeki and Aziz Pahad. These talks originated in a meeting in October 1986 in London, which was set up by Anthony Sampson and David Astor, between Tambo and leading members of the British business establishment, including the chairmen of Courtaulds, Barclays Bank, Sainsbury's, British Petroleum and Rio Tinto-Zinc. Among the people present was Michael Young, a relatively junior executive of Consolidated Goldfields, a notably conservative London-based gold mining company. Young was impressed by Tambo's speech and asked to keep in touch. They met again at a larger meeting between British business leaders and ANC leaders in London in June of the following year. Young was again impressed by Tambo's speech, which took as its theme the need for ordered change. He asked Tambo what was the most useful thing he could do to help the ANC. Young later recalled Tambo and his response: 'He was short in stature with horn-rimmed spectacles that framed his warm brown eyes. His look was kindly but shrewd and he carried an avuncular air that put one at ease and yet enlisted respect.

'I had extended my hand while putting my question to him. He took and held it for what seemed an eternity as he looked at me intently and thought about his reply. We remained silent for some time, holding hands, with him looking into the near distance. His eyes returned to mine and he asked if I could help build a bridge between the ANC and the Afrikaners close to the government.'

Young then spoke to the chairman of his company, who promised to fund such contacts. He also indicated, however, that if the talks became publicly known, he would deny all knowledge and Young would be fired. The latter made contact with two Stellenbosch-based academics with government contacts, Willie Esterhuyse and Sampie Terreblanche. Tambo suggested Aziz Pahad and Tony Trew as the ANC representatives for the first meeting, which took place in October 1987 at the Compleat Angler, a public house on the Thames at Marlow. Tambo was also fully aware of the need for secrecy and did not inform either the London office of the ANC, which was known to be penetrated by the South African security agency NIS, or the NEC that the talks were going to take place.

Authorisation from the South African side to continue the talks after the first meeting came from P.W. Botha through Niël Barnard, the head of NIS. Tambo sent Thabo Mbeki to the second meeting, indicating that he took the talks very seriously. Young thought that Tambo saw them as in some way parallel to the conversations that Mandela was beginning to have with representatives of the government, including Barnard, in prison. These talks, which became known from their later venue as the Mells Park talks, continued intermittently until June 1990 – four months after the release of Mandela and the unbanning of the ANC.

Face-to-face talks in Switzerland between Mbeki, Jacob Zuma, by then head of ANC intelligence, and senior NIS agents emerged from these talks and took place before the release of Walter Sisulu and the other Robben Island prisoners – with the single exception of Mandela – in October. These meetings, and the releases, occurred after Tambo's stroke in August 1989, but he must have been aware that they were in the offing.

By May 1989, Tambo and the NEC realised that there was an urgent need to spell out the ANC's views on negotiations in the light of the implementation of United Nations Resolution 435 on Namibia, pressure from Margaret Thatcher, and the danger that F.W. de Klerk, who had become leader of the National Party in February, and who was to succeed P.W. Botha as president in August, might seize the initiative. Using the communications facilities of Vula, Tambo wrote to Maharaj, who was underground in South Africa and in direct contact with leaders of the MDM: 'The race for who'll control developments in our country has started in earnest & we should be in the lead ... We need to evolve a kind of "435" for South Africa, formulated by us (ANC and MDM), sold to the F[ront] L[ine] S[tates], and used to control and channel pressures, including M[argaret] T[hatcher] & co, that we take charge of what needs to be done in our country.'

A deputation to Lusaka from the UDF and COSATU in June came away with the impression that the ANC was under strong pressure from the USA, the UK, the USSR and China, as well as the Front Line States, especially

Zambia, to enter into negotiations. The Front Line States had indicated that if the ANC did not reach a negotiated settlement, it would have to fight the war against apartheid from within the country. Kaunda had indicated that he was prepared to talk to De Klerk.

The Harare Declaration

A meeting of the OAU in Addis Ababa in July considered a draft document on negotiations and gave the ANC two weeks to come up with a finished declaration. President Kaunda provided an aircraft in which a small team, led by Tambo and including Mbeki, spent a week travelling around the Front Line States, including Zimbabwe, Tanzania, Angola and Botswana, collecting comments, criticism and support for the draft. The most cogent advice came from Julius Nyerere, who warned them that they should bear in mind that, while they had not been defeated by the apartheid regime, neither had they defeated it.

The draft declaration was considered by a meeting of the NWC before submission to a meeting of the Front Line States in Lusaka on 10 August and to a meeting of the OAU's ad hoc committee on southern Africa in Harare on 21 August. The document, which became known as the Harare Declaration, was then approved by a meeting of the Non-Aligned Movement in Belgrade in September and by the United Nations General Assembly in December. The declaration acknowledged that, given goodwill on the part of South Africa, there was the possibility of a negotiated settlement. Speaking in the name of the OAU, it stated: 'We would therefore encourage the people of South Africa as part of their overall struggle, to get together to negotiate an end to the apartheid system and agree on all the measures that are necessary to transform their country into a non-racial democracy.' It went on to lay down the principles that should underlie a new dispensation for South Africa, steps that the apartheid regime should take to create a climate for negotiations, and a programme of action for the OAU itself.

The gaining by the ANC, as 'the liberation movement', of international support for its own document on negotiations was Tambo's crowning diplomatic achievement. He had worn himself out in the process and had a disabling stroke on 9 August – shortly after his return to Lusaka from the tour of the Front Line States and two long meetings of the NWC. Zanele Mbeki, who accompanied the party for some of its journey, gave an account of Tambo's crushing workload. 'He participated fully in the detailed drafting process the night before the trip … When he got to Zimbabwe the next day he was preoccupied with the diplomatic and logistical details, seeking and confirming flights and landing permission for the borrowed plane; personally reconfirming appointments with regional heads of state. At 4 a.m. when all were fast asleep, he called me to reconfirm various logistical arrangements for the next stop in Angola. I don't think that he slept that night.'

Tambo was not present at the meeting of the Front Line States on 10 August and President Kaunda arranged for him to be flown out to London on 11 August in Tiny Rowland's (and Lonrho's) private jet. He then spent five months in the London Clinic before transfer to Sweden for convalescence in January 1990.

By an ironic coincidence, P.W. Botha was removed from the presidency of South Africa in the same week that Tambo had to step down from the leadership of the ANC. Tambo's withdrawal to London left what Joe Slovo called 'a gaping hole' in the leadership of the ANC, which only began to be filled after the release of Nelson Mandela in February 1990 and his assumption of Tambo's old post – that of deputy president. Alfred Nzo acted for a while as the convener of a presidential committee, but he did not have the stature or authority of either Tambo or Mandela. Tambo had, for reasons of security, kept Nzo and the NEC in the dark on many issues. He had not fully informed them about Operation Vula, the Mells Park talks, or the progress of Mandela's talks with Niël Barnard – an issue over which both he and the MDM had some anxiety.

It had been an astonishing achievement on Tambo's part, with the help of Thabo Mbeki and a few others, to keep so many diplomatic balls in the air at one time. He had also had to contend with the pressures that were exerted on the ANC by the Front Line States in 1988–9.

MK had been compelled to leave Angola for Uganda at the beginning of 1989 and there had also been pressure to reduce the ANC population in Zambia. Furthermore, he had to intervene, with the help of the Reverends Frank Chikane and Beyers Naudé, in a conflict inside South Africa between Winnie Mandela and the MDM. The death in December 1988 of Johnny Makatini, head of the International Department, the ANC's long-time representative in the United States and one of Tambo's closest friends and allies, had also come as a blow.

Speaking at Makatini's vigil in Lusaka, Adelaide Tambo had given a clear warning of the dangers that the ANC's peripatetic leaders, especially her husband, faced from overwork and exhaustion. Some time after his death, she recalled that he had been fitted with a pacemaker in the German Democratic Republic a few months before his stroke, but had been unable to return there for a mandatory check-up because of the urgent need to complete the Harare Declaration.

8

Tambo's style of leadership

Oliver Tambo once said of himself that people should understand that in his job as leader of the ANC in exile he had to be not so much 'all things to all people' as 'many things to many people'. It was this protean – kaleidoscopic – quality that makes him a difficult person to pin down or to sum up. He placed himself as near as he could to the ANC's centre of political gravity. As a Christian socialist he was better able than most to hold the balance between the liberation movement's nationalist and socialist/communist wings. He also sought to maintain an ethnic balance within the ANC. Albie Sachs recalls that he never failed to link the Sotho-Tswana equivalent 'matla' with the Xhosa–Zulu cry 'amandla' – power. In terms of the Cold War he was able to appeal equally to Western social democrats and Eastern (or at least Soviet) communists. He came to be seen as epitomising the view of the ANC as a 'broad church', which was open to people of all racial or ethnic groups and most political persuasions. As he told the Kabwe Conference, he subscribed to the founders' view of the ANC as a 'parliament of the people'.

This book should have demonstrated, however, that he had reached this position as the result of a slow and sometimes painful process of evolution. Beginning his political life in the ANC Youth League in the mid-1940s as an 'Africanist', a 'sharp' nationalist, and an anti-communist, it took him a decade to reach the 'broad church' position. He then played a leading role in holding the inclusive line against the 'Africanists' who formed the PAC in 1959. But he continued to take a cautious line in relation to the SACP and the Cold War. He was sceptical about the turn to armed struggle and tried hard for three years, as he explained to the British Parliament in 1985, to get Western support for the ANC in exile before turning to the USSR in 1963.

Working very closely with two African communists, Moses Kotane and J.B. Marks, he refused to allow the SACP, which was not recognised in either country, to organise cells in Tanzania or Zambia until after the Morogoro Conference in 1969. And even then, the Party was not permitted to organise within MK – something that it began to do clandestinely in the late 1970s in the Angolan camps.

Tambo's reticent and low-key – almost anti-charismatic

– demeanour led some people to think that he was weak, a puppet. In his book *External mission* (2012), the late Stephen Ellis went so far as to say that Tambo was 'the perfect frontman, since he was not a communist, his manner was disarmingly mild, and he could generally be relied upon to deliver whatever speech was put in front of him by his aides, of whom Thabo Mbeki was the most important'.

Nothing could be further from the truth. Zanele Mbeki provided an eyewitness account of the real nature of this speech-writing partnership. 'Thabo and OR would sit talking for hours on end – before speechwriting began. Thabo would be mainly absorbing the gist of OR's message … OR was very careful with his language. He did not like jargon in his speeches and therefore would not hesitate to return a draft four or five times for the correction of words and formulations. If inappropriate formulations appeared the speech would be typed all over again. The "delete" and "insert" technology of the computer age did not exist. The to and fro of draft rewrites required a dedicated team of drivers, typists and proofreaders.'

Thabo Mbeki himself recalled: 'Many a time I had to live with the embarrassment of OR completely rejecting my draft texts and, on a number of occasions, using his own notes to deliver addresses radically different from the draft speeches I had prepared.'

Zanele Mbeki has observed: 'OR was never larger than life. His greatness did not overwhelm. He remained a very ordinary human being.' But several people have commented on his inner core of steel. Referring to his relationship with Kotane and Marks in Tanzania in the 1960s, and reflecting on events at Kongwa, Ben Turok commented: 'Oliver was soft in relation to an individual face to face, and in relation to moving a person from one job to another, he didn't kick people out, but he went along with authoritarianism, and implemented it himself. So when you say he's soft, you mustn't get a feeling of a man who's sort of jellyish, he's not. Oliver has a very hard streak in him, very tough.'

Gillian Slovo, daughter of Joe, also commented on the man whom she credited with holding the ANC in exile together in the face of huge pressures: 'One of the most important things that I discovered from knowing Oliver Tambo is that modesty and gentleness are no signs of weakness. OR was one of the kindest and least boastful men I have ever encountered, and yet, you could tell when you were with him that there was steel within.'

Tambo is justly given credit for holding the ANC in exile together and enabling it to come through without major splits, but to what extent should he also be held responsible for the failings of the ANC in exile, including the poor conditions in the Angolan camps, the excesses of the Security Department, the executions, and the prolonged detention of 'suspects' in shocking conditions at Quatro?

He was in some ways a reluctant leader who always

sought consensus – to carry the NEC with him – so there had to be collective as well as individual responsibility. He was noted, above all else, for his ability to listen to a debate and to sum it up, giving weight to all the participants. In Mac Maharaj's view: 'OR had mastered the techniques of how to get people to address the same problem and how to bring the best out of them and get them to work together. He could preside over meetings of forty people, very strong-willed people, and steer them in such a way that by the time he summarized the meeting's consensus, he managed to include everyone.

'For the ANC in exile, far from home, this ability to bring everyone together and hold them together with a common vision was vital. Every individual had to feel that he or she was personally important to the struggle. OR kept them all in the fold and convinced them that we were moving forward. He never allowed the process to degenerate into recrimination or despair. OR had honed these skills to an extraordinary degree. There were times when we thought he should have been more decisive or taken a more radical position. But then you remembered how he was holding the movement together and taking it forward.

'I saw OR in moments of firmness, in moments of anger, but I never saw him being unfair. In debates, he was very sharp, but he never humiliated anyone. He was a man whose leadership you could not doubt because you could see that he gave everything of himself …

'OR held the ANC together for twenty-five years, in part because the NEC would defer matters to him, and he would find a way to work through a problem. That was his uniqueness. Indeed, many members of the NEC were in the habit of relying on him to take care of things. His presence was taken for granted. In that sense, he was irreplaceable.'

Chris Hani had a similar view. He thought that Tambo was a natural and instinctive democrat. 'I think we ought to learn a lot from his general and basic attitude. He never berates, he never shouts at you. He never prescribes. He feels that things should be treated by debate, by arguments, by persuasion. He is a persuasive leader naturally.'

Hani admired Tambo's ability to take personal criticism, and thought that the tolerance of internal criticism, which he had demonstrated in exile, was something that the ANC's leaders should carry with them into the future. He also thought, however, that Tambo moved too slowly on the question of abuses in the camps, on 'incorrect methods of interrogation and handling of suspects and agents', and on conditions at Quatro. But he conceded that 'OR is a person who wants to study a phenomenon first, who does not want to make rash judgements, because I think he would like any judgement to stand the test of time. He has a mind which says let me get all sides of this story.'

Hani thought that it was relatively easy for someone like himself to say: 'Act immediately. I know there are rogues in the security … But OR was saying, look, I have lost men and women as a result of the activities of agents. I have to account to the people of South Africa for what I did about their children. As a movement what means were taken to protect our cadres … You have to remember that lots of cadres died because of information given to the security police, of leaks and everything …

'Ultimately the person responsible is the head of the organisation. So OR could not be as brash as me and Pallo Jordan and others.'

Thabo Mbeki, who worked more closely with Tambo than anyone else, sympathised with his predicament and the impossible task he faced. He did not think that Tambo could be held personally responsible for the abuses in the camps: 'In practice this was not an OR problem. Someone like OR has to deal with millions of things – to do with struggle, international struggle … organisation. The information about abuses came to the leadership quite late because it was dealt with by the military structure, including intelligence …'

But, perhaps, as Joe Slovo pointed out, the real problem was the lack of talent at the top. A few people, including Tambo, Thabo Mbeki, Mac Maharaj, Chris Hani and Slovo himself, had to do too many jobs. Tambo had to delegate important and difficult tasks to people who were not always capable of performing the duties with which they had been entrusted, but it was never easy to find suitable replacements.

Given the stresses and strains of Tambo's role as the international face of the ANC, as someone who was in continuous intercontinental movement for most of three decades, it is hardly surprising that he was unable to maintain day-to-day control of all aspects of the organisation. In truth, he was not cut out to be, and never really aspired to be, a military leader. But he was extraordinarily good at making himself accessible to rank-and-file members of the ANC, at listening to the problems of individuals, and he went out of his way to meet everyone who arrived in Lusaka with first-hand news from South Africa. Zanele Mbeki, a professional social worker, remembered 'his patience, his humanity, the way he agonised both about substantive political issues as well as about mundane concerns of the ordinary membership in the Lusaka ANC community. He would respond to their general but frustrated welfare needs and help to solve non-political problems including purchasing a supply of nappies.'

At one point Joe Slovo approached Ronnie Segal and suggested that he beg Tambo to make himself less accessible. When Segal did as he was asked, Tambo guessed at once that it was Slovo who had put him up to it – and he replied with a polite 'no'.

Hinterland: religion and culture

Among Tambo's great strengths was his 'hinterland' – his deep religious faith and his love of music and song.

Ben Turok recalled how anxious he was to restore to working order a tape that he had himself made of choral music on a visit to St Peter's Basilica in Rome – he had had an audience together with Sam Nujoma of SWAPO with Pope John Paul II in 1982.

Zanele Mbeki gives a good account of these religious and musical dimensions, recalling her attendance with Tambo on Founder's Day at his daughter's Anglican boarding school in the south of England. 'Upon arrival we joined all parents at the opening devotions at the school chapel. I was amazed at how familiar OR was with the English High Church rituals and hymns. Knowing that he had just arrived from revolutionary Lusaka or Morogoro, I had expected the chapel environment to be alien to him; and here was this person who suddenly just blended in. He followed the prayers and music with ease and enjoyment. He even joined in with the English anthem "God Save the Queen". And right there was, you know, Tambo the "priest".

'To me, OR the revolutionary leader of the ANC, the leader of MK, did not translate into a priest. It did not bring to mind a spiritual being. Hence the surprise when, suddenly, you find that the leader of all these firebrand revolutionaries is such a humble, pious, priestly man.'

The contrast between Tambo's mild, donnish manner and the 'terrorist' label, which was pinned on him by the apartheid regime, was one that he sometimes exploited. Addressing a dinner hosted for him and Huddleston in support of sanctions by Sir 'Sonny' Ramphal, secretary-general of the Commonwealth, at Marlborough House in London in 1987, he began his speech: 'I am a terrorist.' After he had addressed a meeting of the British Council of Churches on the same theme, its president, the Archbishop of Canterbury, Dr Robert Runcie, thanked the organiser 'for allowing us to meet a remarkable terrorist'. Albie Sachs recalled his apologetic response to a pacifist heckler at a meeting at Friends House (the Quaker headquarters in London) soon after the Wankie Campaign in 1967: 'We believe in peace, and yet we are becoming killers.'

Tambo's firm friendships with people like Archbishop Trevor Huddleston and Canon John Collins, who were strongly committed to the anti-apartheid cause, but who were not themselves members of the ANC, were of great importance to him. They were among the few people in whom he could really confide. Diana Collins recalled that she had never heard the parable of the Good Samaritan read so well as by Tambo at the memorial service for her husband in St Paul's Cathedral in 1983. He drew strength from an annual retreat at Mirfield in Yorkshire, the home of the Community of the Resurrection. Horst Kleinschmidt of IDAF and Mike Terry of the AAM recalled how important Huddleston's friendship and support were to Tambo during his convalescence in London in 1990.

Tambo's love of music and song, and his role as a

choirmaster and an arranger, were of great importance to him personally. But he was also strongly supportive of a wide variety of initiatives in the spheres of the arts and culture – not only music, but poetry and the graphic arts. He was a close friend of the poet Mazisi Kunene, ANC representative in London, and author of *Emperor Shaka the Great*, and corresponded with him about poetry. He strongly supported the poetic work of Lindiwe Mabuza, who became the ANC representative in Sweden, and a promoter of the tours of the Amandla Cultural Ensemble, which was recruited, with Tambo's support, from the Angolan camps by the jazz trombonist Jonas Gwangwa in the late 1970s. He also encouraged the Mayibuye Cultural Ensemble in London, which was set up in 1975.

As he told the poet Wally Serote, who was involved in the promotion, with the artist Thami Mnyele, of the Medu Art Ensemble, and the Culture and Resistance Symposium and Festival of South African Arts in Botswana in 1982: 'Arts and Culture is very important. It has the potential to unite all South Africans.' In the same year the ANC's Arts and Culture Department was, with Tambo's encouragement, established under the leadership of Barbara Masekela. It was to become one of the most dynamic of the movement's departments. Among the highlights of Tambo's musical and cultural life was his participation in June 1988 at London's Wembley Stadium, with a galaxy of international stars, including Stevie Wonder, Whitney Houston and George Michael, in the Mandela seventieth birthday concert – it was beamed around the world by the BBC.

Family, women and children

Another source of strength was, of course, Tambo's family. Although he often went for many months without seeing them, and could not usually spend more than a few days at a time with them in London, they were of great importance to him. Zanele Mbeki, who spent time with the family in London, was a great admirer of Adelaide Tambo's 'selfless struggle ... bringing up her children virtually on her own while also doing political and diplomatic work'. 'She had very high hopes for the children. She placed them in expensive private schools. Asked why she should do this when there were less expensive state schools, she said, "When I am in England where I can get the best education available for my children, why should I settle for less? In South Africa I could not do this." In between her jobs and family responsibilities, Sis Adelaide constantly received international envoys and British anti-apartheid missions while also participating in the ANC programmes.

'Sis Adelaide was an activist in her own right and she played this role effectively. But by choosing to raise the children and look after the family, her children and other ANC members, she was making it possible for OR to be the leader he was.'

Pauline Webb, a neighbour and friend of Adelaide

Tambo and her 'boisterous' family, a founder of the World Council of Churches Programme to Combat Racism, and later head of religious broadcasting at the BBC, was certain that 'Oliver's recognition of Adelaide's gifts accounted for his own affirmative attitude to women'.

In Tambo's report to the NEC in 1979, he had said: 'We can't afford to exclude half the population from our struggle.' In his closing speech at the end of the first national conference of the ANC Women's Section in Luanda in 1981, he had emphasised 'that the mobilisation of women is the task, not of women alone, or of men alone, but of all of us, men and women alike, comrades in struggle'. He also insisted that 'we should stop pretending that women in our movement had the same opportunities as men'. There were at first relatively few supporters of women's liberation among the men in the NEC – apart from Tambo himself, Mbeki and John Nkadimeng – but there was a gradual shift during the 1980s towards the view expressed by Tambo in 1985 that 'South Africa would not be free so long as women were oppressed' and, later on, that there could be 'no national liberation without women's liberation'.

His concern for children, to whom he had devoted an important part of his life as a teacher, was most forcefully expressed at the IDAF conference on Children, Apartheid and Repression in South Africa, which was chaired by Archbishop Huddleston in Harare in 1987. Dedicated to the issue of the detention and torture of children, it was attended by many people, including young people, who had travelled from South Africa for the event. After reading Ingrid Jonker's poem 'The child is not dead', Tambo went on to say: 'We cannot be true liberators unless the liberation we will achieve guarantees all children the rights to life, health, happiness and free development, respecting the individuality, the inclinations and capabilities of each child.' It would be necessary to attend to the welfare of the millions of children whose lives had been stunted and 'turned into a terrible misery by the violence of the apartheid system'.

Political vision

Oliver Tambo was much more than an astute diplomat and a shrewd political operator with a deep religious and cultural hinterland. Holding the ANC in exile together was a great achievement, but he also developed a clear vision of a future non-racial South Africa. As Albie Sachs has pointed out: 'He was the greatest exponent in our struggle, both in words and action, of a deeply-based and inclusive African nationalism that defined the enemy not in terms of a racial community but in terms of an oppressive system of racial domination.'

Tambo made his vision clear in an interview in London with Anthony Heard of the *Cape Times* in November 1985: 'What we hope our white compatriots will learn to understand is that we don't really see them as whites in the first instance. We see them as fellow South

Africans … They are as good as black. In fact, let us say, they are Africans. We see them as Africans. We are all born there in that country … We live on this continent. It is our country. Let us move away from these distinctions of Europeans and non-Europeans, whites and non-whites … Everyone's property is secure. Everyone's home is secure. The culture is secure. We believe our cultures will begin to merge. We have got a rich variety which, when it comes together, is really going to be something we can put out to the world … Let us not look at one another's colour. Let us not address that. Let us see one another as fellow citizens.'

His vision of South Africa's political future was most clearly spelled out in the instructions he gave in January 1986 to the committee that drew up the ANC's constitutional guidelines. Albie Sachs, a member of that committee, has observed: 'If you did a paternity test on our Constitution it would be his DNA that would come up … responding to constitutional proposals being made inside and outside South Africa, all based in varying degree on group rights and power-sharing between different ethnic communities, he saw common citizenship in a united country with an entrenched Bill of Rights based on democratic values as the answer to what were called minority fears; similarly, at a time when variants of single-party states, military dictatorships and people's power democracies were to be found all over Africa, he unequivocally supported multiparty democracy for South Africa.'

He had a strong sense of humanity, justice and fair play. There were serious problems and human rights abuses in Angola in the early 1980s, but under his leadership the ANC at the Kabwe Conference established a code of conduct that outlawed torture and established procedural rights for persons accused of violating the norms of the movement. He campaigned relentlessly not only for sanctions against apartheid, but also for international pressure to secure the release of all political prisoners, especially Nelson Mandela. Above all, as Albie Sachs has pointed out, he showed that 'it was possible for a totally dedicated freedom-fighter leading a revolutionary struggle to have a courteous and caring nature and display generosity, open-mindedness, integrity and honesty'.

9

Last days, 1990–93

After a visit to Lusaka in January 1990, where they attended an extended meeting of the NEC, Walter Sisulu and the other Rivonia Trial prisoners, accompanied by Thabo Mbeki, travelled to Sweden to pay their respects to Oliver Tambo. It was while they were there that F.W. de Klerk announced on 2 February 1990 the unbanning of the ANC and the release of Mandela. After visits to Zambia, Tanzania, Zimbabwe and Algeria, and attendance at Namibia's independence celebrations, Mandela followed them to Sweden to pay his respects to Tambo at the end of March. He had been elected deputy president of the ANC in Lusaka, but he rejected Tambo's appeal to him to take over as president.

Tambo had another stroke in April 1990, but he soon returned to his family home in London. In December it was decided that he was well enough to return to South Africa for the ANC's national consultative conference.

He travelled with his family by way of Zambia, where he visited President Kaunda and met the still substantial ANC exile population. He arrived at Jan Smuts Airport, Johannesburg, on 13 December to be greeted by Mandela and the largest crowd that had ever gathered there to welcome anyone.

Bob Hughes, chairman of the Anti-Apartheid Movement, had wondered whether Tambo was fit to travel, but Adelaide Tambo reassured him: 'Oliver has to go home; that is what he wants more than anything else.' His health recovered rapidly in South Africa and he was able to deliver a two-hour speech to the ANC congress in Durban in July 1991, during which he gave a detailed account of his stewardship of the ANC over thirty years in exile. It was then that he formally handed the presidency to Mandela and that he was himself elected to the honorific post of national chairman.

Adelaide Tambo told Hughes: 'From the moment he got on the plane he got stronger and stronger; you could almost see the connections being made in his head. The joy of returning home, the exhilaration of returning home was a magical healing process.'

He had an office at Shell House, which he attended regularly in the mornings. He was able to travel within South Africa and was in demand as a speaker at public meetings. He was also able to introduce his children to his Pondoland home and paid a three-week visit to Holy Cross Mission, which was in many ways his spiritual home. In October 1991 he was installed as chancellor of Fort Hare University. On 11 April 1993 he was deeply shocked by the assassination in Dawn Park, Boksburg, of his younger comrade Chris Hani. He and Walter Sisulu arrived together on the scene soon after Hani's death. He attended the funeral house every day, and then, on 19 April, the long funeral service at the FNB Stadium and the burial at Germiston. This was the last occasion on which he appeared in public and met old friends including Mandela, Sisulu and Kaunda. He became ill a few days later and died in hospital in the early hours of 24 April – he was in his 76th year.

Tambo's funeral took place in four parts, a requiem mass and memorial service on 30 April at St Mary's Cathedral in Johannesburg; and then a funeral service at the FNB Stadium, and interment at Wattville, Benoni, two days later. At the cathedral, Archbishop Desmond Tutu celebrated the requiem mass, Archbishop Trevor Huddleston delivered the sermon, and Charles Nqakula read the eulogy. During the memorial service Walter Sisulu and the Reverend Beyers Naudé delivered addresses. The service concluded with the singing of the Reverend Tiyo Soga's great isiXhosa hymn 'Lizalis' idinga lakho Thixo wenyaniso' – God of truth fulfil your promise.

Archbishop Huddleston had concluded his sermon: 'The best memorial for him is free and fair elections for a truly democratic constituent assembly in the shortest time possible.' And he then quoted from John Bunyan's *Pilgrim's progress*: 'When the day that he must go hence was come, many accompanied him to the riverside into which as he went he said "Death where is thy sting?" And as he went down deeper he said "Grave where is thy victory?" So he passed over and all the trumpets sounded for him on the other side.'

At the stadium on 2 May, there was a much smaller, and a more tranquil, crowd than the angry one that had packed it on the occasion of Chris Hani's funeral two weeks previously. Kenneth Kaunda and Jesse Jackson were there, as were many members of the diplomatic corps, but the British ambassador was notable for his absence. Nelson Mandela gave an elegiac address and the Reverend Frank Chikane also spoke. Comparing Tambo with Moses, he said: 'He took us with him to the top of the mountain from where we can see the Promised Land. No one will stop us from reaching it.'

Acknowledgements

I am grateful to Professor William Beinart, the
Leverhulme Trust and the African Studies Centre,
Oxford University, for sponsoring, funding and hosting
much of the research work on which this book, and
my earlier book *The Lusaka years: The ANC in exile
in Zambia, 1963–94* (Jacana Media, 2013), and my
earlier contributions to the Jacana Pocket biography
series, on Chris Hani and Jack Simons, are based. I
would like to repeat my thanks to all the people who
are acknowledged in the earlier books. I have also to
acknowledge two books on which I have drawn a great
deal, Luli Callinicos's *Oliver Tambo: Beyond the Engeli
Mountains* (David Philip, 2004), and Pallo Jordan's
collection of interviews and reminiscences, *Oliver
Tambo remembered* (Pan Macmillan, 2007). I have
also drawn on my earlier research in the ANC archive,

and on the Tambo papers, at Fort Hare University, on the Jack and Ray Simons papers at the University of Cape Town, and on the Phyllis Naidoo papers at the University of KwaZulu-Natal. I am also grateful to the Bodleian Library, Oxford, for access to the papers of Trevor Huddleston and Anthony Sampson, and to the Archbishop of Canterbury's Lambeth Palace Library for access to the papers of Canon John Collins.

I am also grateful to Judge Albie Sachs and the Reverend Mongezi Guma for helpful comments on the manuscript and to Lucy Graham for hospitality and support.

Bibliography

Bernstein, Hilda, *The rift: The exile experience of South Africans*,
    London: Jonathan Cape, 1994

Bernstein, Rusty, *Memory against forgetting*, Johannesburg: Viking,
    1999

Bizos, George, *Odyssey to freedom*, Johannesburg: Random House,
    2007

Braam, Conny, *Operation Vula*, Johannesburg: Jacana Media, 2004

Bunting, Brian, *Moses Kotane: South African revolutionary*, London:
    Inkululeko Publications, 1975

Callinicos, Luli, *Oliver Tambo: Beyond the Engeli Mountains*, Cape
    Town: David Philip, 2004

Commonwealth Secretariat, *Mission to South Africa – The
    Commonwealth Report: The findings of the Commonwealth Eminent
    Persons Group in southern Africa*, Harmondsworth: Penguin, 1986

Ellis, Stephen, *The external mission: The ANC in exile, 1960–90*,
    Johannesburg: Jonathan Ball, 2012

Ellis, Stephen, 'The genesis of the ANC's armed struggle in South
    Africa, 1948-61', *Journal of Southern African Studies*, 37, 4 (2011)

Fifth Summit of East and Central African States, *Manifesto on southern
    Africa*, Lusaka: Government Printer, 1969

Gerhart, G.M., and C. Glaser (eds.), *From protest to challenge, vol. 6:
    Challenge and victory, 1980–90*, Bloomington: Indiana University
    Press, 2010

Gevisser, Mark, *Thabo Mbeki: The dream deferred*, Johannesburg:

Jonathan Ball, 2007

Hassim, Shireen, 'Nationalism, feminism and autonomy: The ANC in exile and the question of women', *Journal of Southern African Studies*, 30, 4 (2004)

Herbstein, Denis, *White lies: Canon Collins and the secret war against apartheid*, Cape Town, HSRC Press, 2004

Huddleston, Trevor, *Naught for your comfort*, London: Collins, 1956

Johns, Sheridan, and R. Hunt Davis (eds.), *Mandela, Tambo, and the African National Congress*, New York: Oxford University Press, 1991

Jordan, Z. Pallo (ed.), *Oliver Tambo remembered*, Johannesburg: Pan Macmillan, 2007

Joseph, Helen, *If this be treason*, London, André Deutsch, 1963

Karis, T., and G.M. Carter, *From protest to challenge, vol. 2, Hope and challenge, 1935–52*, Stanford: Hoover Institution Press, 1973

Karis, T., and G.M. Carter, *From protest to challenge, vol. 3, Challenge and violence, 1953–64*, Stanford: Hoover Institution Press, 1977

Karis, T., and G.M. Gerhart, *From protest to challenge, vol. 5: Nadir and resurgence, 1965–79*, Bloomington: Indiana University Press, 1997

Kasrils, Ronnie, *Armed and dangerous: My undercover struggle against apartheid*, London: Heinemann, 1993

Limb, Peter (ed.), *A.B. Xuma: Autobiography and selected works*, Cape Town: Van Riebeeck Society, 2012

Luthuli, Albert, *Let my people go*, London: Collins, 1962

Macmillan, Hugh, *Chris Hani*, Johannesburg: Jacana Media, 2014

Macmillan, Hugh, *Jack Simons: Teacher, scholar, comrade*, Johannesburg: Jacana Media, 2016

Macmillan, Hugh, 'Oliver Tambo: Beyond the Engeli Mountains (review)', *Transformation*, 61 (2006)

Macmillan, Hugh, 'The "Hani Memorandum" introduced and annotated', *Transformation*, 69 (2009)

Macmillan, Hugh, *The Lusaka years: The African National Congress in exile in Zambia, 1963–94*, Johannesburg: Jacana Media, 2013

Maharaj, Zarina, *Dancing to a different rhythm*, Cape Town: Zebra Press, 2006

Mandela, Nelson, *Long walk to freedom*, Randburg: MacDonald Purnell, 1994

Mandela, Nelson, *No easy walk to freedom*, London: Heinemann, 1966

Matthews, Z.K., *Freedom for my people: Southern Africa, 1961–68* (with a memoir by Monica Wilson), Cape Town: David Philip, 1981

Ngcobo, Lauretta, *Prodigal daughters: Stories of South African women in exile*, Scottsville: University of KwaZulu-Natal Press, 2012

O'Malley, Padraig, *Shades of difference: Mac Maharaj and the struggle for South Africa*, London: Viking, 2007

Pogrund, Benjamin, *How can man die better: The life of Robert Sobukwe*, Johannesburg: Jonathan Ball, 2006 (first published 1990)

Pogrund, Benjamin, *War of words: Memoir of a South African journalist*, New York: Seven Stories Press, 2000

Reddy, E.S. (ed.), *Oliver Tambo and the struggle against apartheid*, New Delhi: Sterling Publishers, 1987

Sachs, Albie, *The strange alchemy of life and law*, Oxford: Oxford University Press, 2009

SACP, *South African communists speak: Documents from the history of the South African Communist Party, 1915–80*, London: Inkululeko Publications, 1981

SADET, *The road to democracy in South Africa, vol. 1, 1960–70*, Cape Town: Zebra Press, 2004

SADET, *The road to democracy in South Africa, vol. 2, 1970–80*, Cape Town: Zebra Press, 2007

SADET, *The road to democracy in South Africa: South Africans telling their stories*, Johannesburg: SADET, 2008

Sampson, Anthony, *Nelson Mandela: The authorised biography*, Johannesburg: Jonathan Ball, 1999

Segal, Ronald, *Into exile*, London: Jonathan Cape, 1963

Sellström, Tor (ed.), *National liberation in southern Africa: Regional and Swedish voices*, Uppsala: Nordiska Institutet, 2002

Sellström, Tor, *Sweden and national liberation in southern Africa, vols. 1 and 2*, Uppsala: Nordiska Institutet, 1999 and 2002

Shubin, Vladimir, *ANC: A view from Moscow*, Johannesburg: Jacana Media, 2008 (first published 1999)

Sisulu, Elinor, *Walter and Albertina Sisulu: In our lifetime*, Cape Town: David Philip, 2002

Slovo, Gillian, *Every secret thing: My family, my country*, London: Abacus, 1997

Slovo, Joe, *Slovo: The unfinished autobiography*, Johannesburg: Ravan Press, 1995

Sparks, Allister, *Tomorrow is another country: The inside story of South Africa's negotiated revolution*, Johannesburg: Struik, 1994

Tambo, Adelaide (ed.), *Preparing for power: Oliver Tambo speaks*, London: Heinemann, 1987

Turok, Ben, *Nothing but the truth: Behind the ANC's struggle politics*, Johannesburg: Jonathan Ball, 2003

Winter, Gordon, *Inside BOSS: South Africa's secret police*, Harmondsworth: Penguin, 1981

Wylie, Diana, *Art and revolution: The life and death of Thami Mnyele, South African artist*, Johannesburg: Jacana Media, 2008

Index